LEAVING CERTIFI

LESS STRESS MORE SUCCESS

Economics Revision

Brian Fogarty

g GILL EDUCATION

Gill Education

Hume Avenue

Park West

Dublin 12

Gill Education is an imprint of M.H. Gill & Co.
www.gilleducation.ie

978 07171 7934 3

Design by Liz White Designs
Artwork and print origination by MPS Limited, a Macmillan Company

The paper used in this book is made from the wood pulp of managed forests. For every tree felled, at least one tree is planted, thereby renewing natural resources.

For permission to reproduce photographs, the authors and publisher gratefully acknowledge the following:

© Alamy: 20, 29, 46T, 46B, 102, 123, 130, 154, 165, 182, 183B;
© DigitalVision/Getty Images Plus: 12; © E+: 35, 71; © Getty Images: 5, 183T, 185; © Independent News and Media: vii; © Inpho: 115; © iStock: 13, 23, 27, 47, 65, 81, 83, 96, 107, 108, 131, 145, 160, 175, 192, 193, 199; © REX / Shutterstock: 1; © Rolling News: v, ix, 120, 177; © Shutterstock: 33, 57, 200; © Wikipedia / Dronepicr: 94.

The authors and publisher have made every effort to trace all copyright holders, but if any has been inadvertently overlooked we would be pleased to make the necessary arrangement at the first opportunity.

CONTENTS

Acknowledgements

For Agata, Jann Caesar and Anja

Introduction

About this book

- In Leaving Certificate Economics, as with other subjects, you should really think of it as two subjects – 'Economics' of course, but also 'How to do well in a Leaving Cert Economics exam'.
- These are not one and the same. You can study a textbook cover to cover, but if you don't follow good technique both on the day and beforehand, you will not maximise your result. Likewise, you can have perfect time management or other areas of exam technique, but if you don't actually 'know your stuff', you'll also fall short of your potential.
- This book is designed to address both. Each chapter carefully sets out what you need to know about that topic, but with an ever-present focus on exam technique and how to approach exam questions.
- The book is divided into an introductory section and 27 chapters:
  - **'About this book'** and **'The exam and how to approach it'** tell you about this book and about exam technique.
  - **Chapter 1** introduces Economics and some basic concepts.
  - **Chapters 2 to 17** cover Microeconomics.
  - **Chapters 18 to 27** cover Macroeconomics.
- At the beginning of each chapter, the main **aims** are listed.
- **Exam focus** boxes appear throughout to help you with exam tips as you go through each topic.

- Particular emphasis is put on **graphs and diagrams**, why they're important and how to draw them correctly.
- At the end of each chapter, you will find a list of the **key points** that were covered.
- Finally, you will see recent **exam questions** covering aspects of each chapter, accompanied by suggested **marking schemes** and **answers** based on the official marking schemes.
- Ultimately, this book attempts to translate Economics into English. When it is explained in simple terms using everyday examples, what at first appears complicated can start to look like what it is – common sense.

The exam and how to approach it

General advice

- It's one thing to study a textbook and 'know your stuff', but without good exam technique you will not maximise your marks.
- **Good exam technique** involves managing your time well in the exam, but it also means reading questions fully and carefully before choosing, composing your answers well, using examples where possible and clearly labelling your diagrams.
- As a rule, spend about **5–10 minutes reading the paper, 25–30 minutes doing the short questions in Section A, and 25–30 minutes on each of your 4 long questions in Section B**. These timing guidelines apply to both the Higher and Ordinary level papers. **Practise** answering past exam questions within these time limits.
- The State Examinations Commission provides **past papers**, solutions and marking schemes for both Higher and Ordinary level on its website, www.examinations.ie. Once you have studied a particular topic, and then wish to attempt a past exam question on it, the **marking schemes** provide an excellent window into how the exam is marked and what is expected. You and your teacher could use a cloud service to share these and other resources between your classmates, reducing duplication.
- **Your Leaving Certificate is a TWO-year course.** Do not postpone your study until the second year. Depending on what your teacher covers first, you will usually have enough material covered in the first year to equip you for 3, if not 4, long questions. So there is no sense waiting until your Leaving Cert year to get down to work.
- However, if you're already in your Leaving Cert year by the time you're reading this, remember that it's **never too late**.
- The exam will contain both Microeconomic and Macroeconomic questions (the contents page tells you which chapters are Micro and which are Macro).
- For **Macro** questions, you will need to have **up-to-date** statistics on the major economic indicators such as inflation, growth, unemployment, government surplus/deficit, balance of payments, the National Debt, etc. Collect the supplements from the major newspapers the day after Budget day, collect exam

supplements, visit sites like www.cso.ie (Central Statistics Office), and – if you cannot find statistics yourself – ask your teacher for help. Your textbook – even this one – is not designed to provide you with current statistics. You must ensure going into your exam that you have familiarised yourself with the latest figures.

Unrivalled Budget 2017 coverage from our team of top writers

- For Micro as well as Macro questions, learning material off by heart will not be enough. In your exam, you will be expected to express **opinions** on current economic events and to back them up with reasons and statistics. It is a good idea to discuss the economy in class, with your classmates and even at home. This develops your critical thinking.

- In the months coming up to the exam, you will also find plenty of articles in the major national **newspapers** giving you an overall picture of the state of the economy, both national and international. You may not understand every word that is written, but if you adopt a routine of reading one or two articles a week, it will add great depth to your Macro answers. There are also weekly current affairs programmes on television that discuss the economic situation as it affects real people's lives. Use social media to exchange useful links with your classmates.

- The formulae for elasticity, national income and the multiplier, etc., can be found in the Sate Examinations Commission's booklet of *formulae and tables*, which you are entitled to use in the exam.

- Don't leave before the end of your exam. You never know what might click with you if you spend those last 30 minutes reading over your answers. One extra sentence could get you another 5 points in your Leaving Cert – walking out with 30 minutes or an hour remaining won't.

- Lastly, knowledge combined with exam technique can get you very far in an exam, but the best way of performing well at either Higher or Ordinary level Economics is to learn to understand and **enjoy it**.

Section A

- This section is worth **100 marks (25%)**. As already stated, you should spend about **25–30 minutes** on this section.
- You will be marked on your **best 6** of the 9 short questions.

- Don't think of Section A as a warm up for the 'real' exam in Section B. It is part of the real exam – a quarter of it. Each question here is worth roughly 4% of your grade in Economics, which could be the difference between a H1 and a H2 or between a H3 and a H4. Give Section A the time and attention that it deserves.
- Note that **5 of the questions carry 16 marks and 4 carry 17**. If you answer all 5 of the 16-mark questions, and only 1 17-marker, your maximum mark will be 97 out of 100. To get 100, you will have to answer all 4 17-markers. The best approach may be to do as many of the 9 as you can, provided you can do so within 25–30 minutes. This implies about 3 minutes per question.
- Many of the questions will require definitions. These will need to be as **precise** as possible.
- Section A questions examine all areas of the course. Previous years' questions give you excellent **practice** for the types of questions that are frequently asked.
- Fill up the spaces provided – when you think you have defined something, write down whatever else you know about it, while keeping within the time. Make sure of the marks.
- If asked to state, don't just give a one-word answer. This will get you only 2–3 marks out of 5. You must use a phrase.
- Where possible, **give examples** even if you're not asked for them, again provided you don't exceed the time.

Section B

- This section is worth **300 marks (75%), comprising 4 questions worth 75 marks (almost 19%) each**. As already stated, you should **spend about 25–30 minutes on each of your 4 questions** from this section.
- There are **usually 3 Micro questions, and usually 5 Macro questions**, which tend to be **more topical**, therefore requiring up-to-date knowledge.
- While there is scope for leaving some chapters out of your study and still having enough covered to allow you to answer **4 long questions**, note the topics that tend to appear most often:
  – Demand, Supply, Elasticity, Costs, Market Structures, and Factor Markets in Micro.
  – The Role of Government, Banking, International Trade and National Income in Macro. Also, the 'History' chapter is often in the last part of a Macro question.
- A careful analysis of past papers is the best way of making decisions about what to concentrate on most. Whatever you do, do not limit yourself to just 4 Macro topics, no matter how many times they have come up in the past.
- Read all the questions first, and all sections of each question before deciding which 4 questions to answer. Do not make your decision based solely on part (a); there will be two or three more sections for you to answer also. Don't choose a question unless you can do all of it.
- **Circle the 'action verb'** in the question. This will remind you as you answer it – along with the marks available – of the type of answer you're expected to give.

If you're asked to explain or discuss, your answer should be much more detailed than if you're simply asked to state.

- Section B questions will usually say how many points to write; **20-markers are usually 4 points at 5 marks each**.

- If you only state, you will get only 2 out of 5 marks. If you correctly explain – preferably with the aid of an example – you can get the other 3 also.

- You should number each point or bullet each point and leave a blank line between each one. The easier it is for the examiner to see what you've written, the easier it is for the examiner to award the marks.

- **Do not write essays**. The examiner will mark your script component by component, so write it component by component. Use bullet points or numbered points.

- Spend about 2 minutes on each point. State, explain and give an example (SEE), then skip a line and move on to the next one.

- **Moving on is important**. There is no sense spending an extra 5 minutes on a question when you could be scoring more marks by spending that 5 minutes on a new question.

Discuss

- When starting a new question, turn to a new page. This makes it easier for the examiner to correct, and also gives you space to come back and add something to a question at the end if you have time. If you need additional space at the end of your answer book, make sure to clearly state what question you are answering.

- As with Section A, **give examples** where possible even if you're not asked for them, but don't exceed the time.

- Similarly, **if you can draw a diagram** to support your answer, draw one even if you're not specifically asked to, but don't exceed the time.

- Draw your diagrams as large as possible. The market structure diagrams in particular are complex, and the intersection of lines needs to be easy to see. Use at least half a page, label every curve and line, and draw all straight lines with a ruler. The easier it is for the examiner to see, the easier it is for the examiner to award the marks. You should **practise** drawing all your diagrams on at least a weekly basis coming up to your exam.

- 'Explain with the aid of a diagram' does not mean 'Draw a diagram but no need to explain'. If you don't accompany your diagram with an explanation of what's happening in the diagram, you get only partial marks.

- If your answer book is full, simply ask for more paper.
- **Avoid any temptation to do a fifth long question in an attempt to cover your bets. Choose your best 4 at the beginning, and use any spare time at the end to go over them and improve on them.**

Differences between the Higher and Ordinary level papers

- Most of the above advice applies equally well to both the Higher and the Ordinary level papers. However, keep in mind the following key differences:
  - Long questions on the Ordinary level paper are broken down into smaller chunks, making it easier to pick up marks. At Higher level, you might be asked to state and explain 4 characteristics for 20 marks. At Ordinary level, it is more common to be asked for 2 definitions for 10 marks and 2 examples or reasons for another 10 marks.
  - At Ordinary level, you are commonly asked to copy diagrams into your answer book and label them. At Higher level, you are expected to draw these diagrams from scratch.
  - While Macro questions on the Ordinary level exam can be quite topical, you are less likely to be asked to *suggest* solutions to problems and more likely to be asked to simply discuss the *effect* of a policy that has already been implemented.
  - In general, the Ordinary level paper does not require the same level of knowledge of the current economic climate. You are commonly given statements and asked to define underlined terms or give examples. At Higher level, you are expected to make arguments for or against a particular course of action and justify them with reasons and statistics.
  - If you feel as you come close to the exam that there is a high chance you will not pass at Higher level, remember that the difference between a H7 and a H8 is 37 points, which is a very steep fall. It may be best in that situation to take the Ordinary level paper instead. A good mark at Ordinary level is better than a fail at Higher level.

1 Introducing Economics

aims

- To define Economics
- To explain the importance of opportunity cost
- To distinguish between a need and a want
- To explain the nature of economic 'laws'
- To discuss the concepts of private cost, social cost, private benefit and social benefit
- To distinguish between wealth, income and welfare
- To distinguish between a positive statement and a normative statement
- To differentiate between Microeconomics and Macroeconomics
- To outline different economic systems

Important economic concepts

First, let's define Economics.

- Economics is what we call a 'social' science.
- A **science** can be defined as an organised body of knowledge. There are many sciences. Physics is an organised body of knowledge and therefore a science, Chemistry is another, and Economics is another.
- A **social science** is one that looks at some aspect of human society. This is how Economics differs from the likes of Biology or Chemistry. They study things; Economics studies people.

- But what aspect of people does Economics study? We can define **Economics** as the study of the production, distribution and consumption of goods and services by society, and how we use our scarce resources, which have alternative uses, to attempt to satisfy our infinite needs and wants.
- While our resources (Capital, Enterprise, Land and Labour) are limited or finite, the needs and wants of mankind are unlimited or infinite.
- A **need** is something that cannot be done without, for example food, shelter or clothing. Our needs are finite.
- A **want** is anything else we might wish to consume once our needs have been satisfied, such as a holiday or a second pair of shoes. Wants tend to be unlimited.
- The concept of **scarcity** is therefore central to Economics. Because resources are limited, this obviously means that some needs and wants will be satisfied while others will not.
- In other words, there are **choices** to be made between alternatives. Economics studies how society makes these choices.
- Whenever there are choices, there is **opportunity cost** – the alternatives that must be done without in order to have that item. If you have only €10, you can go to the cinema or buy phone credit, but not both. If you buy phone credit, the cinema trip is the opportunity cost. If a firm has €1m, it can open a new store in Galway or Dublin but not both. If a government has €500m, it can build a road or a hospital but not both. Opportunity cost affects individuals, firms and governments. Just like scarcity, it is central to Economics.
- All sciences attempt to develop a series of laws to describe what they are studying.
- When studying people, the laws that are developed can be generally true, but will not always be true, as in sciences such as physics. In a given set of circumstances, we can say that most consumers will probably behave in a particular way, but we cannot be 100% sure, e.g. when the price of petrol rises, consumers won't necessarily buy less of it. When taxes are raised, government revenue may fall rather than rise.

exam focus

The concepts of needs, wants, scarcity, choice and opportunity cost run through the entire Economics course, and therefore should inform your thinking at every stage. Never forget these definitions no matter what chapter you are studying.

exam focus

Just because economic laws are not as clear-cut as other kinds of laws, that does not make Economics any less of a science. It simply tells us how unpredictable human beings are. This should be kept in mind as you study the course, particularly the need to always take the circumstances into account.

Deduction and induction

- Economic laws are derived in two ways:
  - The **deductive method** reasons from the general to the particular.
    - ▸ If something is true in general, does that mean it's true in a particular case?
    - ▸ For example, all apples are green, therefore if I buy an apple it will be green.
  - The **inductive method** reasons from the particular to the general.
    - ▸ If something is true in a particular case, does that mean that it's generally true?
    - ▸ For example, the apple I just bought is red, therefore all apples must be red.

Private and social costs and benefits

- A private cost is the cost paid by the person using a good or service, e.g. 80,000 people at a concert.
- A social cost is the cost paid by the rest of society whether they want to or not, e.g. the noise pollution and litter endured by nearby residents.

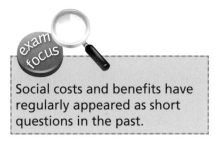

exam focus

Social costs and benefits have regularly appeared as short questions in the past.

- A private benefit is the benefit received by a person for selling a good or service, e.g. the money received by a construction company for building a motorway.
- A social benefit is the benefit received by the rest of society, whether intended or not, e.g. less traffic congestion in nearby towns.

Wealth, income and welfare

- **Wealth** is a stock of assets already accumulated.
- **Income** is the amount of wealth produced by a person or a community over a period of time, normally a year.
- To distinguish between income and wealth, imagine a person in a large house who has lost their job. They might be wealthy, but they have very little income. Or, imagine a person from a poor background who lands a job as a movie star. He might have high income, but for the moment he has very little wealth.
- To accumulate wealth, you need to earn income over time, usually several years. But to earn income, you sometimes need wealth first, e.g. a major coffee shop chain cannot earn millions in profits without first building up its branch network.
- **Welfare** is defined as the overall well-being of a person. Income and wealth can help increase it, but they are not the same thing. Welfare also includes intelligence, health and happiness, which cannot be directly bought or sold.

Positive and normative statements

Economists are concerned with making positive statements rather than normative statements:

- **Positive statements** are statements of fact supported by evidence. They're not made up of opinions, just facts. These can assist consumers or firms or governments to make their decisions.
- **Normative statements** are expressions of opinion. It is not up to the economist to offer their opinion or to make economic decisions. That's up to the government or the individual consumer or firm, hopefully based on positive statements.

For example, the core positive statement of Economics is that people are self-interested. Economists don't, however, make normative statements about whether people should or should not be self-interested. It is a view based on evidence of how people *do* behave, not an opinion on how they *should* behave.

Microeconomics and macroeconomics

Economics is divided into two parts:

- **Macroeconomics** (macro means 'large') studies the decision-making process of government as it relates to such topics as income, employment, inflation, the balance of payments, international trade, growth, etc.
  - It is concerned with broad aggregates.
  - It doesn't deal with the behaviour of individuals.
- **Microeconomics** (micro means 'small') studies the decision-making process of individual units in the economy, at the level of the individual consumer, supplier and producer.
  - It is concerned with how supply and demand determine the quantity of individual goods that will be produced and at what price.

In some ways, Microeconomics and Macroeconomics are like two different subjects. Micro emphasises the motivation of the individual unit; Macro looks at the job of the government and the broad aggregates.

Economic systems

- A **free enterprise** economy is characterised by very little if any government intervention. Property and the factors of production are privately owned, prices are decided by the interaction of supply and demand, and producers are motivated by self-interest and profit. The government only exists to defend the country and to mediate disputes between citizens. Free enterprise does not exist in its pure form, but countries such as the US are often described as free market.

- Advantages include the freedom and choice it gives to consumers, that it allows people to keep the rewards of their own efforts, and that it rewards efficiency and innovation.
- Disadvantages include inequality between rich and poor, success and failure in life is often judged by what you or other people own or earn, vital services will not be provided if they are not profitable to run, the emergence of large multinationals that can squeeze out smaller local suppliers, and a cycle of booms and recessions rather than steady predictable growth.

● A **centrally planned** economy is characterised by the public ownership of the factors of production. The government decides what is produced, how much and at what price. The benefits are allocated according to need, not ability. Cuba is an example of a centrally planned economy.

- **Advantages** are that vital services are provided even if they don't make a profit, wealth is more evenly distributed, people are less prone to comparing what they have with what others have, they make what they have last longer, the black market that arises rewards resourcefulness, and duplication is reduced because the government is a monopolist.
- **Disadvantages** are that there is often an equality of poverty rather than wealth. Absence of a profit motive leads to inefficiency and a lack of innovation. There is also no reason why a government should be better at deciding what to produce than producers and consumers themselves. There is less variety, and frequent shortages of even basic necessities. Central planning has often been associated with a denial of individual freedom.

- A **mixed economy** tries to incorporate the best of both free enterprise and central planning, e.g. the Irish government lets supply and demand decide the price of things like potatoes and furniture, but is heavily involved in the provision of education and health services that may not be provided otherwise. There are many varieties of mixed economy around the world. Economic policy can never be perfected, only improved.

- Definitions of Economics, scarcity, needs, wants, choice and opportunity cost
- Difference between the deductive and inductive methods
- Definition of private and social costs and benefits
- Discussion of wealth, income and welfare
- Difference between positive and normative statements
- Definitions of Microeconomics and Macroeconomics
- Differences between free enterprise, centrally planned and mixed economic systems

2015, Section A, Question 1
Outline why 'choice' is fundamental to the study of economics.

Marking scheme
- The student had to refer to limited resources, unlimited wants, and choice
- 8 + 4 + 4 marks
- 16 marks in total

Answer
In Economics, our resources (Land, Labour, Capital and Enterprise) are limited in supply. They are scarce or finite and they have alternative uses. By contrast, our wants are unlimited or infinite. Therefore, we are forced to choose, and when we do so we face opportunity costs.

2014, Section A, Question 1
Define the term 'opportunity cost'. State one example of an opportunity cost facing the Irish Government.

Marking scheme
- 8 marks for correct definition
- 8 marks for an appropriate example
- 16 marks in total

Answer

Opportunity Cost is the alternative you must do without. If you had two choices, but only enough money for one, the choice not taken represents the opportunity cost.

Examples of opportunity costs facing the Irish government:

- Deferring a hospital extension to build a motorway
- Postponing a tax reduction to increase child benefit
- Paying off the national debt instead of increasing public sector pay

2014, Section A, Question 9

Outline two possible social costs and two possible social benefits of an investment by Eirgrid in upgrading Ireland's electricity network by erecting high-voltage power lines (pylons).

Marking scheme

- 2 social costs + 2 social benefits
- 5 marks + 4 marks + 4 marks + 4 marks
- 17 marks in total

Answer

Social costs:

- Pylons are visually unappealing and can hence negatively impact tourism in areas of natural beauty
- Alleged health effects of electromagnetic fields
- Potential negative effect on farming and on natural habitats
- Fall in the price of both land and houses in areas close to the pylons

Social benefits:

- Greater security in the electricity supply
- More competition in the market may lead to lower electricity prices
- Opportunities within the renewable energy sector
- Increased capacity of renewable energy

exam focus

In this case, you get 5 marks for your first point, whether it's a social cost or a social benefit.

PART ONE

Microeconomics

2 Demand and the Consumer

aims
- To define demand
- To outline the assumptions concerning consumer behaviour
- To discuss the characteristics of an economic good
- To explain the demand function

Introduction

Demand refers to the quantity of a good that the market (i.e. consumers) are willing to buy at any given market price over a period of time. It is more than just a desire to have something, it is an actual willingness to buy it. We call this 'effective demand'.

- **Individual demand** refers to the different quantities one consumer is prepared to buy at each price. This can be represented as a list of prices and quantities called a **demand schedule**, or it can be graphed as a **demand curve**.

- **Market (aggregate) demand** is the total combined quantity that all consumers are prepared to buy at each price. This can also be represented as a demand schedule or as a demand curve.

exam focus

In this chapter, every mention of 'price' is a reference to the price *charged by the seller*. In the chapter on supply, 'price' will mean the price *offered by the buyer*. In equilibrium, these two prices will be the same.

- The decision-making unit that buys goods and services is called the **consumer**.

- They earn four types of income in exchange for providing the four factors of production:
  - **Rent** in exchange for **land**
  - **Interest** in exchange for **capital**
  - **Wages** in exchange for **labour**
  - **Profit** in exchange for **enterprise**

- Those who do not earn income receive transfer payments such as Jobseeker's Benefit. **Transfer payments** are payments made to individuals for which no factor of production is received in return.

Assumptions about consumer behaviour

In Economics, we make the following **assumptions** concerning consumer behaviour:

- Demand depends on **income**. Income – no matter how large it is – is still limited.

- But even though income is limited, a consumer's wants and needs are not. Therefore, he/she must **choose** between those wants and needs they want to satisfy and those they must forego. Opportunity cost exists.

- Consumers are assumed to be **rational** in how they spend their limited income, i.e. they follow their own self-interest. In reality, they frequently make hurried decisions based on limited information, or purchase items for short-term benefit at the expense of their long-term interests.
- They are also assumed to spend their income to achieve the maximum utility. **Utility** is defined as the satisfaction or benefit (it can be one or the other or both) that comes from the consumption of a good or service. A unit of utility is called a **util**.
- Utility is a subjective concept. It is not measurable, and it varies from person to person. Even for one person, it varies over time.
- Consumers are assumed to spend their money only on **economic goods**, i.e. ones with the following **three** characteristics:
  - It gives **utility** or satisfaction.
  - Its demand is greater than its supply, i.e. it must be relatively **scarce**.
  - It must be **transferable**, i.e. it must be possible for one person to sell it to another. For this reason, we don't consider intelligence, patience, etc. to be economic goods.

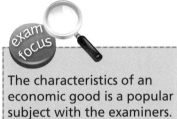

The characteristics of an economic good is a popular subject with the examiners.

- The **Law of Diminishing Marginal Utility** is assumed to operate. This states that as extra units of a good are consumed, the utility gained from each extra unit (the marginal or extra utility) will eventually start to be less than for the last unit.
  - It only applies after a point called the **origin**, i.e. after a certain quantity has been consumed, e.g. if you like cheesecake, you are unlikely to be satisfied after just one mouthful.
  - It assumes income remains constant.
  - It assumes a relatively short time lapse between units, otherwise the effect wears off.
  - It doesn't apply to medicines or addictive products.
- The **marginal utility** is defined as the extra utility or satisfaction gained from consuming one extra unit. As more units are consumed, the marginal utility falls.
- **The Law of Equi-marginal Returns**: In order to maximise his/her utility, a consumer will spend his/her income in such a way that the ratio of marginal utility to price will be the same for all the goods he/she buys. This is because with €1 left to spend, the consumer will buy the good or service that has the highest marginal utility in exchange for that euro.

$$\frac{MU1}{P1} = \frac{MU2}{P2}$$

If this didn't hold, then it would be possible for the consumer to get more utility out of their income by spending their last euro on a different good.

Other demand terms

- **Functional demand**: When people buy goods to consume or use them, e.g. buying a house to live in it.
- **The bandwagon effect**: Buying goods because others are doing so, e.g. buying a brand of phone because your friends have it.
- **Impulse buying**: Buying on the spur of the moment, e.g. buying a coat because its price is reduced, though you had no plans to buy a coat at all.
- **Composite demand**: When a consumer demands a product for more than one use, e.g. water is used for cooking, washing clothes, showering, etc.
- **The paradox of value (diamond/water paradox)**: Even though some products, such as water, are more useful than others, such as diamonds, diamonds still command a much higher price. This is because the marginal utility of one diamond, which is a commodity low in supply, is perceived to be greater than the utility of one unit of water, which is plentiful.

The demand function

- The Demand Function is as follows:

$$Dx = f(Px, Ps, Pc, Y, t, E, Cr., U, G)$$

- This means that demand for any good (called Good X) depends on (or is a function of):
  - The **price** of the good itself (Px)
  - The price of **substitute** goods (Ps)
    - **Substitute goods** are alternative goods that serve much the same purpose as Good X does. The producers of the two goods are therefore competing against each other, and the consumer is likely to choose whichever one is cheaper.

- The price of **complementary** goods (**P***c*)
  - **Complementary goods** (joint demand) are goods that are consumed whenever Good X is consumed, e.g. golf balls and golf clubs, or shoes and shoelaces.
- The **income** of the consumer (**Y**).
  - For a **normal good**, the higher a consumer's income, the more of that good/service they will demand and vice versa, e.g. pairs of shoes.
  - For an **inferior good**, the higher their income, the less of that good/service they will demand and vice versa, e.g. shoe repairs. An inferior good is not necessarily low quality.
- The **tastes** of the consumer (**t**), e.g. as a result of a successful advertising campaign.
- The consumer's **expectations** (**E**). This refers to what the consumer thinks will happen in the future, e.g. a consumer may think that the price of cigarettes or petrol will go up in the Budget, they may decide to buy more cigarettes or petrol **now** before that price increase happens.
- The availability of **credit** (**Cr**). We sometimes cannot buy things unless we can borrow money to do so, e.g. a new car.
- **Unplanned factors** (**U**). An unexpected event can lead to a change in demand, e.g. losing your job.
- The actions of the **Government** (**G**). Sometimes a change in tax or a change in the law will cause more people or fewer people to buy a good even though there has been no change in its price, e.g. compulsory NCT test.

exam focus

In your exam, the price of substitute goods and complementary goods will not be graded as separate points. They are considered to be 'other goods', even though their effects are different.

- If the price of the good itself (**Px**) changes, *ceteris paribus* (all else being equal) there is a movement along the demand curve, i.e. if the price falls, more is demanded and if the price rises, less is demanded. This relationship between price and quantity is called the **Law of Demand**, and it results in a downward-sloping demand curve.

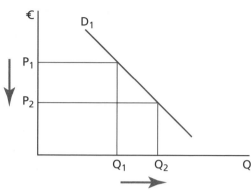

- There are, however, some exceptions to the Law of Demand:

  – **Exclusive demand**: Buying goods (snob/ostentatious goods) because you like knowing that you can afford them while others cannot, e.g. a designer handbag. As they rise in price, most people buy fewer of them but 'snobs' buy more. Of course, not everyone who buys these goods is motivated by exclusive demand.

  – **Speculative demand**: Buying goods in the hope that they can be resold later for a profit, e.g. shares on the stock market. As the price rises, more are bought and vice versa.

Even though we use the term 'curve', the line in the diagram is a straight line. In your exam, you may be given a straight line, a curved line or a kinked line. Once it is downward-sloping, it obeys the Law of Demand.

  – **Giffen goods**: In poor countries, people tend to spend 90% of their income on necessities such as rice, and the other 10% on other goods, for example meat. If the price of rice goes up, people have less money left over after buying rice. As a result they can no longer afford meat, so they therefore buy more rice. All Giffen goods are inferior goods but not all inferior goods are Giffen goods.

- A change in any of the *other* factors in the Demand Function, apart from the price, will cause the demand curve to **shift** either to the right (an extension in demand) or to the left (a contraction in demand).

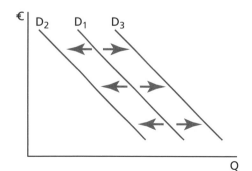

It is vital to remember that a change in the price of the good itself causes a movement **along** the demand curve while a change in any of the other elements of the Demand Function causes the demand curve to **shift**.

- – If the demand curve shifts to the left, this means that **less** is being demanded even though the price is unchanged.
  - – If the demand curve shifts to the right, this means that **more** is being demanded even though the price is unchanged.
- The following factors will cause the demand curve to shift to the **left**, i.e. cause **less** to be demanded even though the price is the same:
  - – A drop in the price of a substitute good (Ps)
  - – A rise in the price of a complementary good (Pc)
  - – A drop in income (Y) if the good is a normal good, or a rise in income if the good is an inferior good
  - – If tastes (t) change away from Good X
  - – If the consumer expects (E) the price to drop
  - – If the Government (G) does something to make it less attractive to buy Good X
- The following factors will cause the demand curve to shift to the **right**, and cause **more** to be demanded even though the price is the same:
  - – A rise in the price of a substitute good (Ps)
  - – A fall in the price of a complementary good (Pc)
  - – A rise in income (Y) if the good is a normal good, or a drop in income if the good is an inferior good
  - – If tastes (t) change in favour of Good X
  - – If the consumer expects (E) the price to rise
  - – If the Government (G) does something to make it more attractive to have Good X

When studying the above effects, always try to think it through rather than just learn it. It takes more effort at the time, but you will remember it for longer and be able to apply it more widely.

The substitution effect, the income effect and the price effect

- The **substitution effect** means that if the price of a good falls, it's now cheaper relative to substitute goods. The substitution effect is always positive, i.e. it causes the consumer to buy more of the cheaper good.
- The **income effect** means that if the price of a good falls, the real (disposable) income of the consumer increases, i.e. if the good is now cheaper, that means the consumer has more money left over. This can give two results:
  - – For normal goods, the consumer will buy more of them.
  - – For inferior goods, the consumer will buy less of them.
- The substitution effect and the income effect combine to give the **price effect**:
  - – It is positive for normal goods, since both the substitution effect and the income effect are positive for normal goods. More is bought if the price falls, less if the price rises.

- It is positive for inferior goods that are not Giffen goods. The positive substitution effect outweighs the negative income effect. More is bought if the price falls, less if the price rises.
- It is negative for Giffen goods, a type of inferior good. The negative income effect outweighs the positive substitution effect. Less is bought if the price falls, more if the price rises.

	Substitution Effect	+ Income Effect	= Price Effect
Normal	Positive	Positive	Positive
Inferior (Not Giffen)	Positive	Negative	Positive
Giffen	Positive	Negative	Negative

key point

- Definitions of demand, individual demand, market demand
- Assumptions concerning consumer behaviour
- The Law of Equi-marginal Returns
- **Dx = f(Px, Ps, Pc, Y, t, E, Cr., G)**
- The Law of Demand
- Exceptions to the Law of Demand
- The substitution effect, the income effect and the price effect

exam Q

2015, Section A, Question 2 (a)
Explain the concept of the Equi-Marginal Principle of Consumer Behaviour.

Marking scheme
- Definition @ 6 marks
- 6 marks in total

Answer
A consumer maximises their utility by spending their money in such a manner that the ratio of marginal utility to price will be the same for all the goods they buy.

2015, Section A, Question 2 (b)

In equilibrium, a consumer buys five bottles of water at €2.50 each and eight bagels at €3 each. The marginal utility of the fifth bottle is 5 utils. Calculate the marginal utility of the 8th bagel. (Show your workings.)

Marking scheme

- 7 marks + correct answer 3 marks

Answer

$$\frac{MU\ W}{P\ W} = \frac{MU\ B}{P\ B}$$

$$\frac{5}{€2.50} = \frac{x}{€3}$$

x = 6 utils (the marginal utility of the 8th bagel)

2014, Section B, Question 1 (a) (i)

Number of units consumed	1	2	3	4	5
Total utility in units/Utils	20	45	60	70	75
Marginal utility in units/Utils	20	25	15	10	5

State and explain the law illustrated in the above table.

Marking scheme

- Statement: 4 marks
- Explanation: 9 marks
- Total: 13 marks

Answer

(i) Statement: This table illustrates the Law of Diminishing Marginal Utility.

Explanation: As a person consumes more units of a good, the marginal or extra utility gained from each extra unit will eventually begin to decline. In the table, this occurs after the second unit, since the utility gained from the third unit is only 15 utils, 10 less than for the second unit.

2014, Section B, Question 1 (a) (ii)

Outline two assumptions underlying this law.

Marking scheme

- 2 assumptions @ 6 marks each
- 12 marks in total

exam focus

SEE – State, Explain and give an Example. 15 marks means 6 minutes. Use bullet points and leave a line between each point.

Answer

- It only applies after a point called the **origin**. Some minimum quantity must have been consumed before utility begins to diminish, e.g. a whole apple rather than a single bite.
- It is assumed that consumers' **tastes** remain stable between units. Their perception of what constitutes utility should not change.
- Consumer **income** is assumed to remain constant between units, ensuring no change in consumption patterns.
- It is assumed that there is no **time** lapse between units which would allow for utility to recover, e.g. you wouldn't travel on a second holiday to New York a week after you had returned from New York, but you may wish to go there again five years later.

2013, Section B, Question 1 (a)

(i) Distinguish between the terms 'effective demand' and 'derived demand'.

(ii) Outline two possible exceptions to the Law of Demand.

Marking scheme

- 1st correct term @ 7 marks (4 + 3)
- 2nd correct term @ 4 marks (2 + 2)
- 2 exceptions @ 7 marks (4 + 3) each

Answer:

(i) **Effective demand** is demand supported by actual purchasing power. It is more than a mere desire to have something, e.g. a private jet.

    Derived demand is when a factor of production is demanded not for its own sake but for its contribution to the production process, e.g. bricks are only demanded for the building of walls.

(ii) **Giffen Goods:** As the price rises, consumers have less income to spend on other goods so they switch consumption to the Giffen goods.

    Snob goods: For those who gain added utility from possessing items they know others cannot have, a price rise may make them more attractive, e.g. a sports car.

    Speculative goods: Price rises may encourage people to buy now so as to avoid further increases, or to profit from them by buying now and selling later, e.g. rare paintings.

    Goods of addiction: If a person is unable to cease consumption of a good, they will continue to buy the same amount even if the price rises, e.g. cigarettes.

3 Supply and the Producer

Introduction

Supply means the quantity of a good that producers are willing to sell at any given market price over a period of time.

- **Individual supply** refers to the different quantities one producer is prepared to sell at each price. This can be represented as a list of prices and quantities called a **supply schedule**, or it can be graphed as a **supply curve**.

- **Market (aggregate) supply** is the total combined quantity that all producers are prepared to sell at each price. This can also be represented as a supply schedule or as a supply curve.

> **exam focus**
>
> In the Demand chapter (Chapter 2), every mention of 'price' was a reference to the price *charged by the seller*. In this chapter 'price' means the price *offered by the buyer*. In equilibrium, these prices will be the same.

- The **Law of Supply** states that as the price offered for a good increases, *certeris paribus* (all else being equal) more of it will be supplied. This will result in an upward-sloping supply curve:

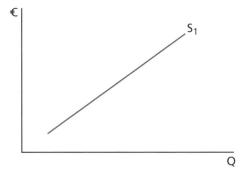

- However, there is a number of other supply curves with which you will need to be familiar:

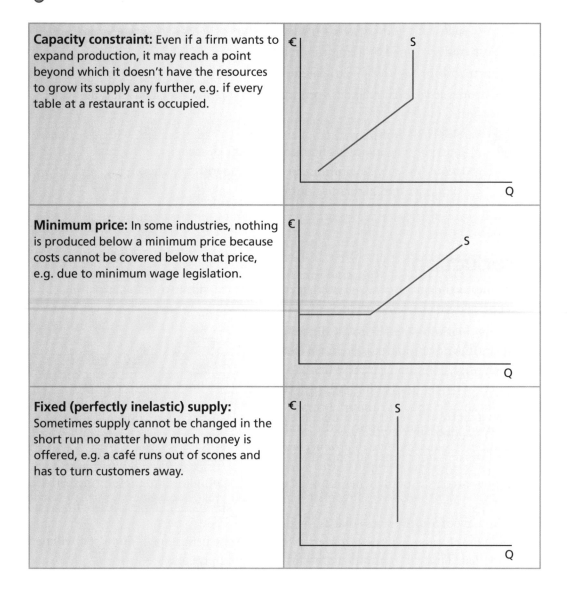

Capacity constraint: Even if a firm wants to expand production, it may reach a point beyond which it doesn't have the resources to grow its supply any further, e.g. if every table at a restaurant is occupied.	
Minimum price: In some industries, nothing is produced below a minimum price because costs cannot be covered below that price, e.g. due to minimum wage legislation.	
Fixed (perfectly inelastic) supply: Sometimes supply cannot be changed in the short run no matter how much money is offered, e.g. a café runs out of scones and has to turn customers away.	

- A **producer** is a firm that sells goods or services in an attempt to satisfy consumer needs and/or wants.
- A **firm** is an individual unit of business that produces output and sells its product to the market (i.e. to consumers) with the aim of making a profit.
- An **industry** is a group of firms that produce the entire output of a particular good, e.g. the mobile phone industry.

- **Private sector** firms are privately owned businesses. There are several kinds:
  - **Sole trader**: owned by a single individual
  - **Partnership**: between 2–20 shareholders
  - **Co-operative**: each member's profit depends on how much business they do with the company
  - **Private limited company (Ltd)**: between 1–149 shareholders, who have limited liability
  - **Public limited company (Plc)**: at least 7 shareholders, no maximum. Shares can be bought and sold on the stock exchange
- **Public sector** firms are semi-state bodies owned by the government, e.g. Bord na Móna.
- The **optimum size** of the firm is reached when **unit cost** is minimised. The optimum size will vary from industry to industry – a hairdresser can survive in business on a few thousand customer visits a year, a tablet manufacturer has to make and sell millions of units in order to keep afloat.

Economies and diseconomies of scale

Internal economies of scale are forces at work inside a firm that lower the unit cost as quantity produced is increased/as the firm increases in size. These forces are:

- **Construction**: It doesn't cost double to build a factory twice the size. This reduces the unit cost.
- **Technical**: Larger firms can spread the cost of expensive machinery over a larger quantity of units, thus reducing the unit cost.
- **Integrated production**: Larger firms have the money to engage in more than one stage of the production process, reducing unit cost.
- **Labour**: Larger firms can engage in specialisation/division of labour. Output per worker is increased, unit cost is reduced.
- **Production**: Larger firms can operate continuous production, without the time and expense involved in stopping and starting, e.g. a medical devices plant that operates around the clock.
- **Raw materials**: Larger firms waste less raw materials. If they're not used in the production of one good, they can be used in another. This reduces unit cost.
- **Financial**: Larger firms have more credibility and are considered less risky by banks and investors. This reduces unit costs.
- **Purchasing**: Larger firms save more than smaller ones when buying in bulk. The bigger the buyer, generally the bigger the reduction the seller will offer on each unit bought.
- **Distribution**: A large firm with lots of deliveries can have lower unit cost than a small firm with fewer deliveries to make.
- **Marketing**: Costs per unit are lower for larger firms, similar to when purchasing raw materials.

Internal diseconomies of scale are forces at work inside a firm that raise the unit cost as quantity produced is increased beyond a certain point/as the firm increases in size. These forces are:

- **Communication**: Larger firms are harder to manage. More information is needed to make decisions, and it's harder to communicate with everyone. Unit costs rise.
- **Boredom/low morale**: As a firm grows and engages in more specialisation of labour, jobs may become more mundane. This reduces productivity. Unit costs rise.
- **Workers' expectations**: The larger the firm, the more likely some workers are to believe it has the money to give in to higher wage demands.
- **Conflict**: In bigger firms, workers may feel unimportant as individuals, leading to industrial relations conflict, etc. This drives unit costs up.
- **Layers of management**: Large companies need more supervisors and clerical staff, who are not directly engaged in production, adding to unit costs.

External economies of scale are forces at work outside a firm that lower the unit cost as quantity produced is increased/as the industry increases in size. They affect all firms in the industry simultaneously. These forces are:

- **Outsourcing**: As an industry grows, new firms are set up to provide such spin-off services as recruitment, training and advertising. They also provide component parts and specialised machinery. Outsourcing allows the firms in the industry to concentrate on their core competencies, reducing their unit cost.
- **Marketing**: As an industry grows, firms come together in trade associations or trade fairs to market their collective output. This reduces unit costs.
- **Sharing**: Firms in larger industries sometimes come together to share the burden of research and development, etc. This reduces unit costs.
- **Government**: As the economy grows, the government can provide better infrastructure, benefiting all firms.

External diseconomies of scale are factors outside a firm that raise the unit cost as quantity produced increases beyond a certain point/as the industry increases in size. They affect all firms in the industry. These forces are:

- **Infrastructure**: As an industry expands, the pressure on a country's infrastructure grows. The government cannot build roads, etc. as fast as output is increasing. Unit costs rise.
- **Raw materials**: As more raw materials are required, they become harder to obtain. The price rises or, alternatively, lower quality raw materials may have to be purchased. Either way, unit costs rise.
- **Labour**: Skilled labour becomes harder to find, so wages rise, or else less skilled workers are hired.

Why small firms can still survive

Despite large firms' economies of scale, small firms often still manage to do very well in Ireland. This is due to:

- **Small market**: Our population of less than 5m people. This may not give large multinationals the economies of scale they need, leaving the market to smaller Irish firms.
- **Transport**: Since Ireland is an island, it is costly to transport many types of goods into the country. This can hand an advantage to home-grown firms.
- **Loyalty and personal attention**: Small firms offer a familiar face to their customers. In close-knit local communities, this favours small local producers.

- **Nature of the product**: Perishable goods and hand-made products may be cheaper to produce locally.
- **Preference for control**: If you own a small business, expanding means sharing control. For this reason, family-owned businesses may prefer to stay small.
- **Finance**: Small businesses cannot expand without capital.

The Supply Function

The Supply Function is as follows:

$$Sy = f(Py, Pr, C, T, U, Cr., G)$$

This means that the supply of Good Y depends on (or is a function of):

- The **price** consumers are offering for Good Y (**Py**).
- The price of **related** goods (**Pr**). **Related goods** are defined as other goods that the producer can offer instead of Good Y, e.g. a pizza company can make either ham

and mushroom or pepperoni pizza. If the price consumers are offering for pepperoni pizza rises, the company will switch some of its limited resources from producing ham and mushroom pizza to pepperoni pizza, **reducing** the supply of ham and mushroom pizza.

- The **Cost of Production (C)**. If the cost of producing Good Y falls, but the price remains the same, the firm will supply more because it's now more profitable, e.g. a fall in the price of a key raw material.
- **Technology (T)**. An improvement in technology can make it possible to produce more of Good Y, e.g. a social media site that allows you to reach more customers. Technology usually doesn't disimprove.
- **Unplanned factors (U)**. These are events outside the control of the producer, and can have either a positive or a negative effect. Two examples are a fire that burns down a factory and therefore restricts production, or, on the other hand, the discovery of a new fuel, which causes the price of oil to fall.
- Availability of **credit (Cr.)**. Firms require credit from banks in order to set up and expand and hence supply the market.
- **Government (G)**. The government can offer incentives to promote a desirable product, e.g. healthy food.

A change in any part of the Supply Function – **except for a change in the price (P _y_)** – will cause the supply curve to **shift** either to the right or to the left.

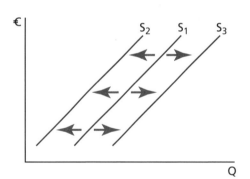

It is vital to remember that a change in the price of the good itself causes a movement **along** the supply curve while a change in any of the other elements of the demand function causes the supply curve to **shift**.

key point

- Definition of supply
- The Law of Supply
- Economies and diseconomies of scale
- Reasons why small firms survive in the Irish economy
- Sy = f(Py, Pr, C, T, U, Cr., G)

2016, Section B, Question 1 (a)

(i) Outline four factors that determine the supply of a good or service.

(ii) Explain the difference between a movement along a supply curve and a shift in a supply curve. Use appropriate diagrams to illustrate your answer.

Marking scheme

- 4 factors @ 5 marks each
- 2 diagrams @ 3 marks and 2 marks
- 2 explanations @ 5 marks each
- 35 marks in total

Answer

(i)

- **Price of the good itself:** The higher the price offered by the consumer, the more will be supplied, provided there isn't a capacity constraint, e.g. as a singer's popularly grows, they hold their concerts in sports stadia rather than in smaller venues.
- **Price of related goods:** If offered more for an alternative good, firms will produce that good instead, e.g. organic food. The supply curve of the original good shifts left.
- **Technology:** New technology allows firms to produce more at the same price, e.g. digital movie cameras have made it easier to produce and release films. The supply curve shifts to the right as technology improves.
- **Unplanned factors:** A positive unplanned factor (e.g. faster production method) will shift the supply curve right, a negative unplanned factor (e.g. a new competitor) will shift the supply curve left.
- **Government:** The government can offer incentives and grants to promote the production of particular products, e.g. bio-fuels. The supply curve shifts to the right.
- **Cost:** If a firm cuts production costs, it can produce more, e.g. cheaper fuel lets an airline offer more routes. The supply curve shifts right if costs fall, left if they rise.

Exam Focus: This answer is an example of how it cannot hurt to use examples even if you're not asked for them – provided you don't go over the time. This 20 marker should take you 8 minutes.

(ii) Movement along a supply curve:

If the price consumers are willing to offer for the good increases, the quantity supplied will also increase. This results in an upward-sloping supply curve, as shown.

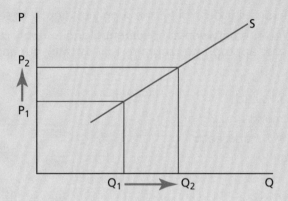

Shift in a supply curve:

If there is a change in any other factor in the supply function, the supply curve will shift either to the left (a decrease in supply) or to the right (an increase in supply).

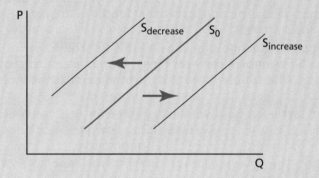

4 Markets and Equilibrium

aims

- To define markets and how they determine prices
- To outline what happens if there is an upward or downward shift in either supply or demand
- To explain all four possible scenarios

Introduction

A **market** exists wherever or whenever buyers and sellers meet to strike a deal, such as a corner shop, an auction, an internet site, a stock market (where shares are traded), a currency market or a commodity market (where oil, copper, gold, etc. are traded).

Some markets are much bigger than others; all involve a similar interplay of demand and supply to determine price.

A market is in **equilibrium** when there is no tendency to change from the current price and quantity.

The **black market** refers to the trading of a good or service without any tax being paid to the government, e.g. illegally smuggled cigarettes.

- **Consumer surplus** is the difference between the highest price a consumer is willing to pay, and what they end up paying, e.g. if Karen is happy to buy a car for €40,000 but gets it for €30,000, her consumer surplus is €10,000.

- **Producer surplus** is the difference between the lowest price a producer is willing to accept, and the price they get, e.g. if Patrick is happy to sell a car for €20,000 but gets €30,000 for it, his producer surplus is €10,000.
- If the buyer's maximum price is lower than the seller's minimum price, no trade can take place.
- If the buyer's maximum price is higher than the seller's minimum price, a **bargaining range** exists between the two points. The final price depends on the bargaining power of the buyer and the seller. In the above example, the bargaining range for Karen and Patrick is between €20,000 and €40,000.

We must also distinguish between:

- **Factor markets** (land, labour and capital are purchased by entrepreneurs to be combined into a business unit)
- **Intermediate markets** (raw materials and partially finished goods are bought for use in making other goods)
- **Final markets** (finished goods are bought by the final consumer)

Supply and demand at work

So how is price actually decided? Through the interaction of supply and demand. We already know what a normal demand curve and supply curve look like. Let's now combine them in one diagram:

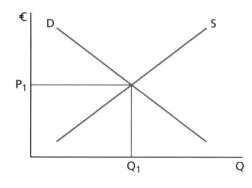

- If the price were below P_1, demand would be greater than supply. Buyers would compete by offering more. Sellers would capitalise on this competition by charging more. As these two factors push the price up, supply and demand would equal where the supply and demand curves intersect. Here, the market 'clears' at price P_1.
- If the price were above P_1, supply would be greater than demand. Sellers would compete by charging less; consumers would capitalise by bargaining and shopping around. These two factors would push down the price until demand and supply equalled where the curves intersect. Again, the market would clear at price P_1.
- Either way, the market mechanism is 'self-correcting', i.e. whenever supply and demand are unequal, they eventually force each other to be equal again. This doesn't always happen as quickly as we would like, and when it eventually does it there can be a painful adjustment, e.g. a slump in house prices.

Changes to the equilibrium

We will now see what happens if the supply or demand curve shifts. A **new** equilibrium will be reached, but in a different place. This rarely happens in some markets but regularly in others, e.g. stock market prices change every minute, the price of bread can stay relatively unchanged for years.

Keep in mind that in reality these four effects often overlap, with several forces acting on supply and demand at the same time. The price we get is the aggregate of these effects.

Four scenarios or cases are possible:

(1) The demand curve shifts left, causing a **fall** in the equilibrium price **and** equilibrium quantity.

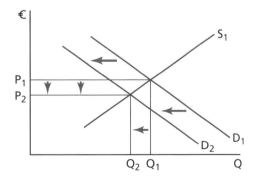

- It can be caused by:
  - A fall in the price of a substitute
  - A rise in the price of a complement
  - A fall in income (normal good), or a rise in income (inferior good)
  - A change in taste away from the good
  - Expectation of a price drop
  - A fall in the availability of credit
  - A government action that lessens demand

(2) The demand curve shifts right, causing a **rise** in the equilibrium price **and** equilibrium quantity.

- It can be caused by:
  - A rise in the price of a substitute good
  - A fall in the price of a complement
  - A rise in income (normal good), or a fall in income (inferior good)
  - A change in taste in favour of the good
  - Expectation of a price rise
  - A rise in the availability of credit
  - A government action that boosts demand

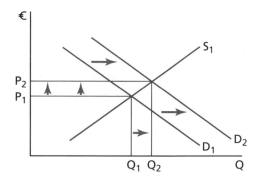

(3) The supply curve shifts left, causing a **rise** in the equilibrium price but a **fall** in the equilibrium quantity.

- It can be caused by:
  - A rise in the price offered for a related good
  - A rise in the cost of production
  - An unfavourable unplanned factor
  - A fall in the availability of credit
  - A government action that lessens supply

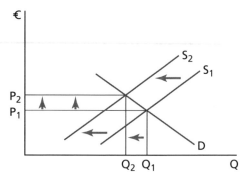

(4) The supply curve shifts right, causing a **fall** in the equilibrium price but a **rise** in the equilibrium quantity.

- It can be caused by:
  - A fall in the price offered for a related good
  - A fall in the cost of production
  - An improvement in technology
  - A favourable unplanned factor
  - A rise in the availability of credit
  - A government action that boosts supply

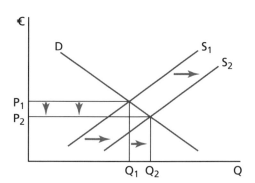

key point

- How supply and demand lead to equilibrium
- The factors that can cause equilibrium to change

exam focus

A rule of thumb:

- When demand shifts, P and Q go in the same direction.
- When supply shifts, P and Q go in opposite directions.

2015, Section B, Question 1 (b)
The market for wheat is in equilibrium. Explain, with the aid of a separate diagram in each case, the effects which each of the following market situations is most likely to have on the equilibrium position for wheat:

(i) Exceptionally wet weather conditions

(ii) An increasing percentage of the population is suffering from wheat allergies and intolerance

(iii) A decrease in the price of oil.

Marking Scheme

- Labelled diagram, including new supply/demand curve @ 5 marks
- Arrow indicating direction of shift @ 1 mark
- Reason for shift @ 2 marks
- New price, new quantity @ 1 mark each
- 10 marks per sub-question, 30 marks in total

Answer

(i) Exceptionally wet weather conditions:

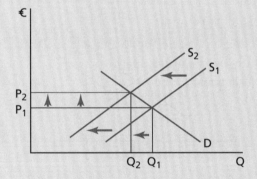

- Wet weather conditions will result in less wheat being grown and supplied to the market.
- Therefore, the supply curve will shift to the left (from S1 to S2).
- Demand is now greater than supply.
- This will drive up the equilibrium price from P1 to P2.
- The equilibrium quantity will fall from Q1 to Q2.

(ii) An increasing percentage of the population is suffering from wheat allergies and intolerance:

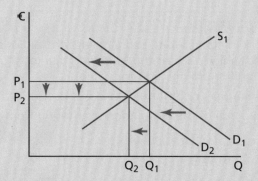

- Consumer demand for wheat products will fall due to allergies and intolerances.
- Therefore, the demand curve will shift to the left (from D1 to D2).
- Supply is now greater than demand.
- This will drive down the equilibrium price from P1 to P2.
- The equilibrium quantity will fall from Q1 to Q2.

(iii) A decrease in the price of oil:

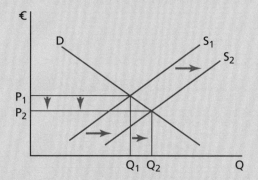

- The cost of producing wheat will fall, so farmers will be prepared to increase their supply.
- Therefore, the supply curve will shift to the right (from S1 to S2).
- Supply is now greater than demand.
- This will drive down the equilibrium price from P1 to P2.
- The equilibrium quantity will rise from Q1 to Q2.

5 Costs, Revenue and Profit

aims

- To differentiate between revenue and profit
- To distinguish between fixed and variable costs
- To distinguish between normal profit and supernormal profit
- To distinguish between the short run and the long run
- To explain the shape of the various cost curves
- To outline the conditions under which profit is maximised

exam focus

This is one of the more technical chapters. Don't expect to get everything the first time you read it. This chapter requires repeated study and plenty of patience. Try to work it through in your mind rather than rote-learn it.

Introduction

In this chapter, we look at the factors that determine how much profit – if any – a firm will make.

$$\text{Profit} = \text{Revenue} - \text{(total) cost}$$

But what exactly is revenue?

$$\text{Revenue} = \text{Price} \times \text{Quantity}$$

So **Revenue** is the number of items sold multiplied by the price charged. You don't get to keep it all of course – you have to pay your costs.

$$\text{Total cost} = \text{Fixed cost} + \text{Variable cost}$$

A **Fixed Cost (FC)** is a cost that must be paid regardless of the number of units sold, e.g. a cinema must pay its rent whether it sells a thousand tickets a night or none at all.

A **Variable Cost (VC)** is a cost that increases as output increases, e.g. the more meals a restaurant serves, the more electricity it uses. So,

$$\text{Profit} = (P \times Q) - (FC + VC)$$

Normal profit and supernormal profit

Normal Profit is the minimum profit necessary to justify staying in business in the long run. The business covers all its fixed and variable costs, and in addition pays just enough profit to the entrepreneur to persuade them to keep the business open. If profit falls below normal profit, the business closes.

Supernormal Profit is any profit over and above normal profit. Even if it falls a little, the business doesn't have to close.

In Economics, we normally assume that a firm is trying not just to make a profit, but to *maximise* that profit. So what quantity should it sell and at what price in order to achieve this? The obvious answer might seem to be: maximise your sales and you will maximise your profit. But this is not so, as we shall see.

The short run and the long run

The **Short Run** is the period of time during which at least one of the four factors of production is still unchanged. A firm may hire more workers, attract more shareholders and rent more land, but if it has not yet built a larger factory or bought extra machinery, it is still in the short run.

The **Long Run** starts as soon as the fourth factor has changed, i.e. all four factors are variable in the long run.

The length of the short run varies from firm to firm and industry to industry. A street merchant could change all four factors in a week; for a multinational technology firm it could take years.

In the short run, firms face fixed and variable costs. In the long run, all costs are variable.

AFC, AVC, SRAC and LRAC

Average Fixed Cost (AFC) is equal to fixed cost divided by quantity sold. In the short run, the more units a firm sells, the lower its AFC.

This is because a fixed amount is being spread over a great number of units, e.g. Sports Shop A and Sports Shop B each pay €1,000 in rent per month. Shop A sells 100 jerseys, Shop B sells 200 jerseys. Therefore, Shop A's AFC will be €10, while Shop B's AFC will be €5. All else being equal, Shop B can afford to charge a much lower price since its fixed costs are spread over a greater number of jerseys.

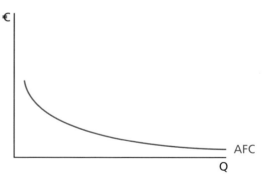

Average Variable Cost (AVC) is equal to variable cost divided by quantity sold. In the short run, it will initially slope downwards much like the AFC curve above. However, as the firm sells more units, it will start to slope back up again.

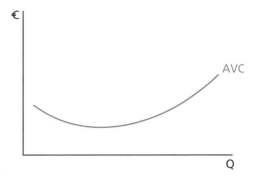

This is because of the **Law of Diminishing Marginal Returns**, which states that as more units of a variable factor are combined with a set number of units of a fixed factor, the output per unit of the variable factor will eventually start to fall. To understand what this means, imagine a restaurant in which the fixed factor is an oven and the variable factor is the number of chefs.

Two chefs sharing an oven can probably produce more than twice as much food as one chef using one oven. Perhaps a third chef's addition to total output would be even greater than the second chef's. However, if we add a fourth and then a fifth chef, but all five share just one oven, the addition to total output of the fifth is very likely to be lower than that of the fourth. This isn't because he's not as good a chef, but simply because all five are trying to use the same oven – the same fixed factor. The addition to total output as a result of adding an extra unit of a variable factor has begun to fall. This drives up average variable cost, giving us a U-shaped AVC curve.

We already learned that total cost is equal to fixed cost plus variable cost. Therefore, **Average (total) Cost** must be equal to average fixed cost plus average variable cost:

$$AC = AFC + AVC$$

This will also result in a U-shaped curve in the **Short Run Average Cost (SRAC)**. This is for three reasons:

- **Greater spread of fixed costs** will cause it to slope down, i.e. a downward-sloping AFC curve will in turn contribute to causing the AC curve to slope downward.

- **Specialisation** will also cause it to slope downward. This means that as output rises, workers can concentrate on one task. As they get better at it, output per worker increases.

- The **Law of Diminishing Marginal Returns** will cause the AVC curve to eventually slope upward, in turn causing the AC curve to slope upward.

In the long run, since all factors change, firms solve the problem of diminishing marginal returns by adding not just more variable factors but more (until now) *fixed* factors. To return to the earlier example, the restaurant purchases another oven so that the chefs no longer have to fight over just one oven. This leads to greater output (Q) at a lower cost, requiring us to draw another short run average cost curve, and then another and another as the firm expands, moving from one short run to the next. However, eventually a point is reached beyond which the addition of more ovens (and chefs) will cause **Average Cost (AC)** to rise again, giving us a U-shaped **Long Run Average Cost (LRAC)** curve.

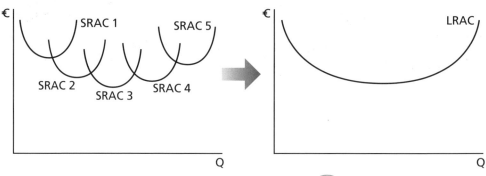

The LRAC is U-shaped for two reasons:

- For lower quantities, **economies of scale** initially outweigh diseconomies of scale (see Chapter 3) and cause it to slope downward. Average cost falls as output increases, e.g. a supermarket can sell milk for less than a corner shop.

exam focus

Note that while the SRAC and LRAC curves are both U-shaped, they are U-shaped for different reasons. If you're asked to explain the shape of one, but give the wrong set of reasons, you'll get no marks.

- As output increases beyond a certain point, **diseconomies of scale** outweigh economies of scale and cause it to slope upward again. Average cost rises as output increases.

The MC curve and the AC curve

Marginal Cost (MC) is the cost of producing one extra unit of output, or the increase in total cost as a result of producing one more unit. In the short run, it initially slopes down, but due to the Law of Diminishing Marginal Returns, it eventually produces an upward-sloping curve.

The **Marginal Cost curve cuts the Average Cost curve upwards at its lowest point**. This is because:

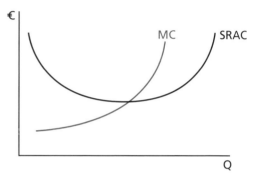

- While MC is lower than AC, AC will be falling.
- While MC is greater than AC, AC will be rising.
- While MC is equal to AC, AC will be constant.

Imagine if one more student walked into your classroom. If the new (marginal) student is taller than the average of the people already there (the 'old' average), then the 'new' average (i.e. the average of everyone *now* in the room) will be bigger. If the marginal student is shorter, the new average will be smaller. If the marginal is the same height as the old average, the new average will be the same as the old average. If you were to graph the results, you would see why the MC curve cuts the AC curve at its lowest point.

AR in the short run and the long run

Average Revenue (AR) is equal to total revenue (TR) divided by quantity (Q) sold. The AR curve is essentially the firm's demand curve, since it shows all combinations of price and quantity.

$$AR = TR/Q$$

In the short run, AR must be greater than AVC. When a clothes shop sells its first pair of jeans of the month, it cannot reasonably hope to pay all of its rent with the revenue earned. That would be one expensive pair of jeans. Therefore, AR doesn't have to be greater than FC in the short run, and hence doesn't have to be greater than SRAC. However, it does have to be greater than AVC. If the AVC (electricity, wages, etc.) of selling a pair of jeans is €50, then the price of the jeans must be greater than €50. Otherwise, what's the point in selling them?

In the long run, AR must be equal to LRAC in order to make a normal profit, and greater than LRAC in order to make a supernormal profit. Remember that in the long run, there are no fixed costs, only variable costs (e.g. rent, while fixed in the short run, varies if you wait long enough). If a business wants to make a supernormal profit and survive in the long run, its total revenue must be greater than its total costs. Therefore, its AR must be greater than its LRAC.

- If AR is lower than LRAC, the firm will make a loss and will have to close down.
- If AR is equal to LRAC, normal profit will be earned.
- If AR is greater than LRAC, supernormal profit will be earned.

Maximising profit

Marginal Revenue is the extra revenue earned from selling one more unit of output. If the MR curve is below the AR curve, the AR curve slopes downward, i.e. to sell more units you usually have to drop your price. (However, we will encounter a case later in the book where AR and MR are horizontal.) Finally, after learning many new cost and revenue terms, we are ready to answer the question of **how a firm can maximise its profit**:

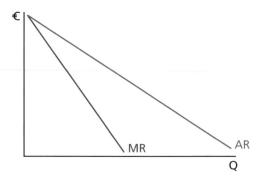

- The answer is that the profit-maximising condition is MC = MR.
- Imagine a furniture firm that sells 50 chairs a week. Wouldn't it prefer to sell 51? Most people would assume that the answer is yes.
- But it depends. If the revenue (MR) earned from doing so is greater than the cost (MC) of doing so, then it makes sense. If not, it doesn't.

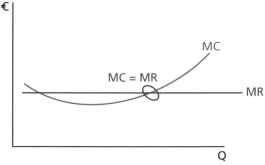

- Remember that since MC is rising, the 51st chair will cost more to produce than the 50th while the 51st will most likely sell for only the same price as the 50th, if not less. So even though extra profit might be earned as a result of selling the 51st, it will be less than the extra profit from the 50th. Essentially, the gap between MR and MC is narrowing.
- The MC for the 52nd will be higher still, while again the price will, if anything, decrease. When a stage is reached that the MC is greater than the MR, it doesn't make sense to sell any more chairs – the extra cost would be greater than the extra revenue.

- Therefore, the firm maximises its profits when MC = MR. If it sold one less chair, it'd make less profit because MR would still be greater than MC, and if it sold one more, it'd make less profit because MC would now be greater than MR.

- As a result, that part of the MC curve that lies above the AVC curve is equivalent to the **short run supply curve**, while that part of the MC curve above the LRAC is equivalent to the **long run supply curve**. This is because these are the lowest points that the intersection of MC and MR can take place in the short run and long run respectively – nothing will be supplied below them.

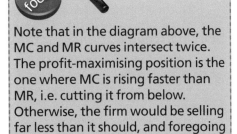

Note that in the diagram above, the MC and MR curves intersect twice. The profit-maximising position is the one where MC is rising faster than MR, i.e. cutting it from below. Otherwise, the firm would be selling far less than it should, and foregoing the profit involved.

key point

- Introduction to all the cost curves.
- A firm must cover its AVC in the short run but all of its costs in the long run.
- The SRAC and LRAC curves are both U-shaped – but for different reasons.
- Profit is maximised when MC = MR, with MC cutting MR from below.

exam Q

2016, Section B, Question 4 (a)
(i) Distinguish between the short-run and the long-run production periods.
(ii) In the short-run firms may stay in the industry even if they are making a loss. Explain this statement.

Marking scheme
- 10 marks for distinguishing (5 + 5)
- Explanation @ 5 marks
- 15 marks in total

Answer
(i) In the SR, at least one of the four factors of production remains constant. In the LR, all four are variable.
(ii) A firm cannot hope to cover its total costs in the SR. But as long as it covers its variable costs, and hence makes a contribution toward its fixed costs, it will stay in business. In the LR, it must cover its total costs to remain in business.

2015, Section B, Question 3 (a)

(a) In the case of any **two** of the following three pairs distinguish between the two concepts:

- Marginal Cost and Average Cost
- Explicit Cost and Implicit Cost
- Normal Profit and Supernormal Profit.

Marking scheme

- 4 definitions @ 5 marks each
- 20 marks in total

Answer

Marginal cost is the addition to total cost of producing one more unit of output.

- **Average cost** is the total cost divided by the number of units produced.
- **Explicit cost** is any direct payment made in the running of a business, e.g. wages, electricity, etc.
- **Implicit cost** is an opportunity cost that does not appear in the accounts of a firm, e.g. if a person gave up a job paying €60,000 a year in order to start a business.
- **Normal profit** is the minimum level of profit needed to justify staying in business in the LR.
- **Supernormal profit** is any profit in excess of normal profit.

2015, Section B, Question 3 (b)

The table below shows the output and production costs for a small bakery.

Units of Bread	Total Costs(€)
0	100
100	200
200	280
300	330
400	360
500	450
600	600
700	770

(i) Use the data in the table above to answer the following questions:

- What are the fixed costs of operating this bakery? Explain your answer.
- What are the variable costs of producing 300 loaves of bread?
- What is the average cost of producing 400 loaves of bread?

(ii) Using the data from the table above, draw one graph showing the following (you may use graph paper to complete this question):
- Total costs (label the curve TC)
- Total variable costs (label the curve VC)
- Total fixed costs (label the curve FC)

(iii) With reference to the graph you have drawn in part (ii) does the graph represent the short run or the long run? Outline a reason for your answer.

Marking scheme
- Fixed cost @ 6 marks
- Variable cost @ 3 marks
- Average cost @ 3 marks
- Labels: Costs / Qty 2 @ 1 mark each = 2 marks
- Graph of total fixed costs @ 4 marks
- Graph of total cost @ 7 marks (2 + 2 + 3)
- Graph of total variable cost @ 7 marks (2 + 2 + 3)
- Reason @ 3 marks
- 30 marks in total

Answer
(i)
- Fixed cost = €100. This must be paid even if nothing is produced.
- Variable cost of producing 300 loaves = €330 − €100 = €230
- Average cost of producing 400 loaves = Total cost/Total output = €360/400 loaves = €0.90

(ii)

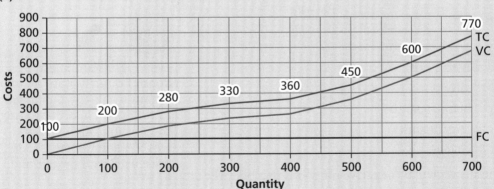

(iii)
The graph must represent the SR since fixed costs only exist in the SR.

- To define and state the formula for all four kinds of elasticity
- To calculate a result from a given set of figures
- To comment on the size and sign of your answer, and advise a producer on any price change they should make
- To identify which type of product a given answer refers to
- To outline the factors affecting elasticity

exam focus

Don't try to rote-learn elasticity. Try to think it through and understand it – it will stay in your head a lot longer. As with many topics in Economics, elasticity sounds more complicated than it actually is.

Price elasticity of demand (PED)

Definition: It measures the degree to which the demand for a good changes in response to a change in the price charged for that good by the producer.

When you divide the proportionate change in quantity by the proportionate change in price that caused it, the size and sign of the answer can assist the producer in deciding whether to increase or decrease the price or leave it unchanged.

Formula: $$\frac{\Delta Q}{\Delta P} \times \frac{P_1 + P_2}{Q_1 + Q_2}$$

exam focus

Even if an exam question doesn't directly state all four required values, you'll need to find them in order to use the formula, e.g. if a bar was 50c and it increased in price by 50%, $P_1 = 50c$ and $P_2 = 75c$.

P_1 = before price
P_2 = after price
Q_1 = before quantity
Q_2 = after quantity
Δ = change

The answer will be **negative** for goods that obey the Law of Demand and **positive** for goods that don't (snob goods, goods subject to speculative demand).

The size of the answer in absolute terms (ignoring the sign) means:

Size of answer	Definition	Meaning	To increase revenue, the producer should:	Effect on profit
= 0	Perfectly inelastic: The demand curve is vertical.	Demand will remain constant regardless of the price. Example: life-saving drugs. 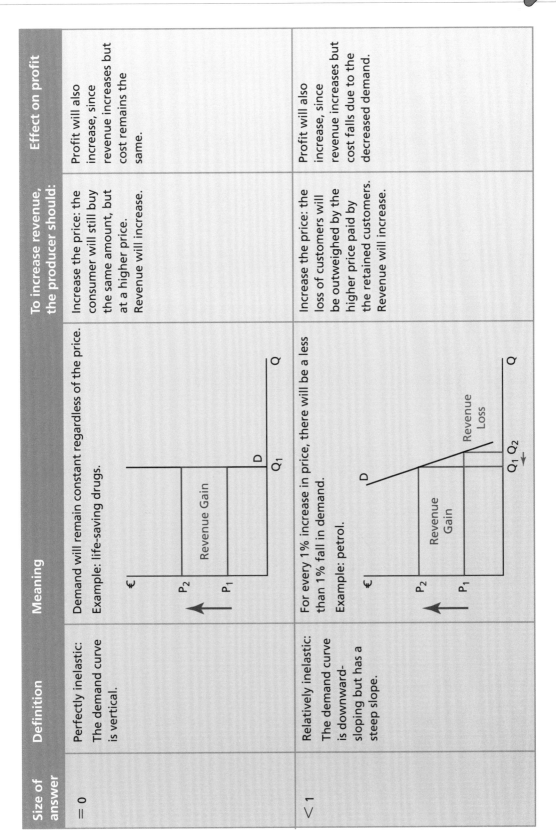	Increase the price: the consumer will still buy the same amount, but at a higher price. Revenue will increase.	Profit will also increase, since revenue increases but cost remains the same.
< 1	Relatively inelastic: The demand curve is downward-sloping but has a steep slope.	For every 1% increase in price, there will be a less than 1% fall in demand. Example: petrol.	Increase the price: the loss of customers will be outweighed by the higher price paid by the retained customers. Revenue will increase.	Profit will also increase, since revenue increases but cost falls due to the decreased demand.

Size of answer	Definition	Meaning	To increase revenue, the producer should:	Effect on profit
= 1	Unit elastic: The demand curve slopes downward at a 45 degree angle.	For every 1% increase in price, there will be a 1% drop in demand. Example: 'necessary luxuries' – goods we don't strictly need but most people are not prepared to do without, e.g. TV. 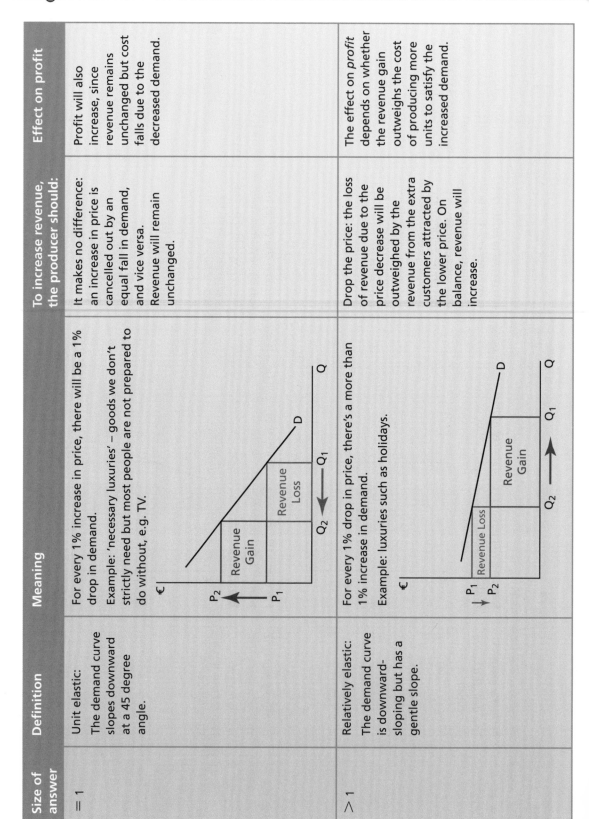	It makes no difference: an increase in price is cancelled out by an equal fall in demand, and vice versa. Revenue will remain unchanged.	Profit will also increase, since revenue remains unchanged but cost falls due to the decreased demand.
> 1	Relatively elastic: The demand curve is downward-sloping but has a gentle slope.	For every 1% drop in price, there's a more than 1% increase in demand. Example: luxuries such as holidays.	Drop the price: the loss of revenue due to the price decrease will be outweighed by the revenue from the extra customers attracted by the lower price. On balance, revenue will increase.	The effect on profit depends on whether the revenue gain outweighs the cost of producing more units to satisfy the increased demand.

Size of answer	Definition	Meaning	To increase revenue, the producer should:	Effect on profit
= ∞ (infinity)	Perfectly elastic: The demand curve is horizontal (as seen in Perfect Competition).	Even a tiny price increase will lead to a 100% fall in demand, because the consumer can get it cheaper elsewhere. Example: homogenous substitute goods such as apples or potatoes. *Graph: demand curve D horizontal at P1/P2, showing Revenue Loss, with axes € and Q, quantities Q1.*	Leave the price the same: increasing the price leads to a 100% drop in demand. Decreasing the price doesn't lead to any increase in demand. Revenue will remain the same.	Profit is unchanged since price and quantity are unchanged. The firm is a price taker.

Price Elasticity of Demand is affected by the following factors:

- **Substitutes**: The more of them there are, the more elastic the demand. In response to a price increase, the consumer can simply buy a different product, e.g. brands of butter.

- **Proportion of income**: The higher the proportion, the more elastic the demand. Consumers are more sensitive to price rises on items taking up a higher proportion of their income (e.g. a new car), less sensitive to price rises on items that take up a small proportion (e.g. a cup of coffee).
- **Durability**: The longer lasting the item, the more elastic the demand. Replacement can be postponed (e.g. a schoolbag).
- **Alternative uses**: the more uses a good has, the more elastic the demand. A price increase may cause a fall in demand in terms of each individual use but a large aggregate fall.
- **Branding and loyalty**: The more effective the advertising campaign is for a product, and the more loyal the consumer is to that product, the more inelastic the demand (e.g. a mobile phone brand).

exam focus

A great way to learn about and understand Elasticity, as with many other topics in Economics, is to always ask 'What will happen if I change this?' Mentally change the price in your head, and think about what you would do if you were the consumer. Economics is all about the domino effect.

- **Degree of necessity**: The less the consumer needs it, the more elastic the demand. If they don't like the price increase, the consumer can simply do without the item (e.g. electric gates).
- **Time**: Over a longer period of time, demand becomes more elastic since substitutes become more available (e.g. electric cars as a substitute for petrol cars).

In relation to PED, you can be asked for the following:

- Definition
- Formula
- Calculate PED from given figures
- Meaning of the sign of the answer
- Meaning of the size of the answer
- Advice as to what a producer should do
- From a given answer for PED, identify the type of good in question
- The factors affecting PED (State, Explain, Example)

Income elasticity of demand (YED)

Definition: It measures the degree to which the demand for a good changes in response to a change in the consumer's income (Y).

When you divide the proportionate change in quantity by the proportionate change in income that caused it, the answer you get tells you a lot about how the consumer views that good.

Formula:

$$\frac{\Delta Q}{\Delta Y} \times \frac{Y_1 + Y_2}{Q_1 + Q_2}$$

Y_1 = before income
Y_2 = after income
Q_1 = before quantity
Q_2 = after quantity
$\triangle$ = change

The answer will be positive for normal goods and negative for inferior goods:

- A **normal good** is one that you buy more of as your income increases, and vice versa.
- An **inferior good** is one that you buy less of as your income increases, and vice versa. 'Inferior' in this case does not refer to inferior quality. What one consumer views as a normal good, another may consider to be an inferior good.

Size of answer	Type of good	Meaning
Normal good with YED < 1	The good is a necessity.	A 1% increase in income causes an increase in demand, but the increase is less than 1%, and vice versa.
Normal good with YED > 1	The good is a luxury.	A 1% increase in income causes a greater than 1% increase in demand for the good, and vice versa.
YED < 0	Inferior good.	An increase in income causes a decrease in demand. If the good is a necessity, the answer will be < 1 in absolute terms (i.e. ignoring the sign).

exam focus

In relation to YED, you can be asked for the following:

- Definition
- Formula
- Calculate YED from given figures
- Meaning of the sign of the answer (normal/inferior)
- Meaning of the size of the answer (luxury/necessity)
- From a given answer for YED, identify the type of good in question

Cross price elasticity of demand (CED)

Definition: It measures the degree to which the demand for Good A changes in response to a change in price of Good B.

When you divide the proportionate change in demand for Good A by the proportionate change in the price of Good B that caused it, the answer can tell you about the relationship – if any – between the demand for those two goods.

Formula:

$$\frac{\triangle QA}{\triangle PB} \times \frac{PB_1 + PB_2}{QA_1 + QA_2}$$

PB_1 = before price of Good B
PB_2 = after price of Good B
QA_1 = before quantity of Good A
QA_2 = after quantity of Good A
 $\triangle$ = change

exam focus

It might at first appear as if you have four different definitions and formulae to learn. But compare them – they're essentially the same but with different factors included.

Answer	Meaning	Explanation
> 0 (positive)	The goods are substitutes. Example: two brands of mascara.	If the price of one increases, the consumer buys more of the other one instead. The larger the figure, the closer the goods are as substitutes.
< 0 (negative)	The goods are complements (in joint demand). Example: badminton rackets and shuttlecocks.	If the price of one decreases, the consumer buys more of the other good (along with more of the first good). If one of the goods is more expensive than the other, the elasticity of the more expensive one will have a greater effect on the elasticity of the cheaper one than the other way round.
= 0	There is no apparent relationship. The goods are neither substitutes nor complements. Example: raspberries and thumbtacks.	A price change for one of the goods has no effect on the demand for the other, either positive or negative.

exam focus

In relation to CED, you can be asked for the following:
- Definition
- Formula
- Calculate CED from given figures
- Meaning of the sign of the answer (substitutes/complements/neither)
- Meaning of the size of the answer (strength of relationship)

Price Elasticity of Supply (PES)

Definition: It measures the degree to which the supply of a good changes in response to a change in price offered for that good by the consumer.

Formula:

$$\frac{\triangle Q}{\triangle P} \times \frac{P_1 + P_2}{Q_1 + Q_2}$$

P_1 = before price
P_2 = after price
Q_1 = before quantity
Q_2 = after quantity
$\triangle$ = change

The answer will normally be positive, since the producer will normally supply more of a product (provided they are able to) if the consumer is willing to pay more for it.

The bigger the answer, the more elastic the supply.

If PES = 0, this means the product is perfectly elastic, i.e. fixed in supply. The supply curve will be vertical.

Price Elasticity of Supply is influenced by the following factors:

- **Availability of specialised factors of production**: If the producer cannot easily hire extra skilled workers or purchase specialised machinery, supply will be inelastic.
- **Full capacity**: If the firm is already making as many units as it can, supply will be inelastic until it can increase its production capacity.
- **Mobility of factors of production**: If a firm can easily switch workers or machines over to the production of a factor that the consumer is willing to pay more for, supply will be more elastic.
- **Time**: Over a longer period of time, supply becomes more elastic. The producer is better able to make the adjustments they need to make in order to increase supply.
- **Nature of the product**: Sometimes production takes place in anticipation of demand, so supply cannot easily be changed, e.g. a sugar crop. In such cases, supply is inelastic (vertical supply curve).

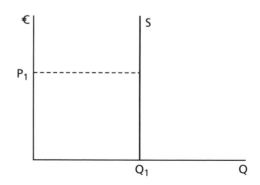

In relation to PES, you can be asked for the following:

- Definition
- Formula
- Calculate PES from given figures
- Meaning of the size of the answer
- Factors affecting PES (State, Explain, Example)

- Definitions of PED, YED, CED and PES
- Formulae for PED, YED, CED and PES
- Calculate all four from a given set of figures

2016, Section A, Question 6

The table below shows the annual average level of income in a country and the corresponding demand for Product A for two years.

Year	Income (€)	Product A (units)
Year 1	57,000	100
Year 2	63,000	200

(i) Calculate the income elasticity of demand (YED) for Product A. Show your workings.

(ii) Using your knowledge of YED, explain the economic meaning of this figure you calculated in (i) above.

Marking scheme

- Calculation @ 9 marks (must show workings)
- 4 marks for stating that it is a normal good
- Explanation @ 4 marks
- 17 marks in total

Answer

(i)

$$\frac{+100}{+6{,}000} \times \frac{€57{,}000 + €63{,}000}{100 + 200} = \frac{+1}{+60} \times \frac{€120{,}000}{300} = +6.67$$

(ii)

- Because the sign is positive, we can say that this is a normal good.
- In fact, because the result is greater than 1 in absolute terms, it's also a luxury good.
- As the consumer's income rose, their demand for the good rose, and rose by a greater percentage than their income did.

2016, Section B, Question 1 (b)

Read the following statements and indicate if they are TRUE or FALSE. Explain your answer in each case.

(i) The cross price elasticity of demand for substitute goods has a negative value.

(ii) Price Elasticity of Demand (PED) tends to be more elastic in the long-run than in the short-run.

(iii) When demand for a good is price inelastic, a reduction in price will increase total sales revenue.

(iv) Income elasticity of demand (YED) for luxury goods is positive.

Marking scheme

- 4 correct statements (true/false) @ 2 marks each
- 4 explanations @ 4 marks
- 24 marks in total

Answer

(i)

- FALSE
- The CED for substitutes is positive, not negative.
- A rise in the price of one causes the demand for the other to rise, e.g. a rise in the price of Crest toothpaste causes more people to buy more Colgate instead.

(ii)

- TRUE
- Given enough time, people can adjust their consumption patterns away from a good that has risen in price, e.g. if petrol rises in price, people still buy it in the SR. In the LR, they can switch to diesel or electric cars.

(iii)

- FALSE
- If PED is inelastic, for every 1% price drop, there will be a less than 1% increase in demand. Revenue will therefore fall.

(iv)

- **TRUE**
- All luxury goods are normal goods. Therefore, as income rises, consumers demand for these goods increase. In the case of luxury goods, the percentage increase in demand is greater than the original percentage increase in income.

2014, Section B, Question 3 (a)

(i) Define the categories of Price Elasticity of Demand (PED): elastic, inelastic and unit elastic.

(ii) State three factors that affect PED and explain how each factor affects it.

Marking scheme
- 3 definitions @ 5 marks each
- 3 factors @ 5 marks each
- 30 marks in total

Answer

(i)

- **Elastic demand:** The percentage or proportionate change in the price of a good results in a *greater* percentage or proportionate change in the quantity demanded of that good, e.g. a 2% price increase causes a 5% fall in demand.
- **Inelastic Demand:** The percentage or proportionate change in price of a good results in a *smaller* percentage or proportionate change in the quantity demanded of that good, e.g. a 5% price increase causes only a 3% fall in demand.
- **Unitary Elastic Demand:** The percentage or proportionate change in the price of a good results in an *equal* percentage or proportionate change in the quantity demanded of that good, a 3% price increase causes a 3% fall in demand.

(ii)

- **Substitutes:** The more close substitutes a good has, the more elastic the demand. The consumer has a greater opportunity to switch if the price of the good increases.
- **Proportion of income:** The more a consumer spends on a product relative to their income, the more elastic the demand. We are more sensitive to changes in the price of cars than we are to changes in the price of bananas.
- **Durability:** The longer an item you already own is likely to last, the more elastic the demand for a replacement. If car prices rise, people will try to make do a little longer with the car they have.
- **Time:** The more time the consumer has in which to adjust, the greater the elasticity. If electricity prices doubled, you wouldn't instantly ask the company to cut you off. But a year later, perhaps you would have had solar panels installed.
- **Alternative uses:** The greater the number of uses a good has, the greater the elasticity of demand. A price rise may cause only a small fall in demand in terms of each use, but the combined fall may cause the good to be price elastic, e.g. the alternative uses of sugar.

7 Introduction to the Market Structures

aims
- To define what a market structure is
- To briefly introduce each market structure and position them relative to one another

The term '**market structure**' refers to the way in which firms behave in any given industry and why. Remember, we assume that all firms are aiming to maximise their profits – but depending on the characteristics of their industry, they will meet varying degrees of success. Just as it's a rare football team that can ignore the opposition, firms cannot ignore the world they live in. The biggest factor will be the number of competitors, and this in turn will be determined by the most important single characteristic of each market structure, **barriers to entry**, i.e. how difficult it is to

exam focus

Economics is easier to understand – and much more enjoyable – if you try to put yourself in the place of the consumer, the firm or the government and ask yourself, 'What would I do to maximise my own outcome if I were in this situation?' That's what they think about, so if you want to understand why they do what they do, that's what you must think about too.

get into the industry. This will in turn influence other characteristics, and hence decide what level of profit a profit-maximising firm can hope to make.

There is a number of market structures that we will examine over the next couple of chapters. Because comparing them with one another makes each one easier to understand, they are best represented on a spectrum like so:

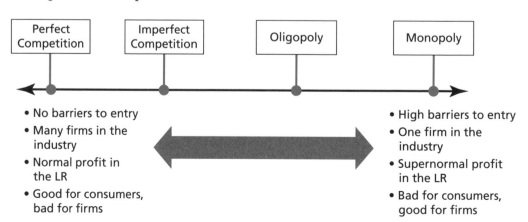

- At one extreme, imagine an industry in which there are literally no barriers to entry at all – anyone who wants to can set up and start selling. It's most likely that if firms make any profit at all in the LR, it will be only normal profit, since they have so many competitors selling identical products. As a result, the consumer benefits in the LR because prices are competed downward. We call this unlikely scenario **Perfect Competition**.

- At the other extreme, if you're lucky enough to be the only firm in an industry, and are able to keep other firms from entering and hence stealing some of your customers, you stand a good chance of making supernormal profits, even in the LR. This tends to be bad for consumers since there they have no choice of producer, and the lack of competition means higher prices and relatively little innovation. We call this situation **Monopoly**. Because it is so bad for consumers, governments usually intervene in the market to break up a monopoly or reduce barriers to entry.

In between these two extremes, we will study two additional scenarios.

- **Imperfect Competition** is similar to perfect competition except that firms sell similar but not identical products. Since no firm's product has a substitute quite like it, imperfect competition is not quite as competitive as perfect competition, and is therefore a step closer to the monopolistic end of the scale. As a result, it's sometimes called **Monopolistic Competition**.

- **Oligopoly** – the most realistic of the market structures – is one in which there are barriers to entry and a small number of producers make up the market. Sometimes they try to act together as a monopolist in order to increase profits, but the element of competition between them doesn't always make this possible. Acting together in this way is called **collusion**. Since it is bad for the consumer, it is illegal, but unfortunately very difficult to prove. Oligopoly is more competitive than monopoly but still more monopolistic than imperfect competition.

As we go through these market structures one by one, the chapters will each follow the same format:

- First, the **characteristic** of the structure will be explained (the 'rules of the game').
- Then we will see how equilibrium is reached in the **Short Run**.
- Third, we will see if there is any change in the **Long Run**. Sometimes there will be, sometimes there won't. It all depends on the characteristics.
- Sometimes there will also be a comparison of two market structures.
- In some cases advantages and disadvantages are given.

We will also study **Price Discrimination**, which involves a firm selling the same product to two different consumers at different prices where the price difference isn't due to a difference in cost. It is not strictly speaking a market structure so hence it doesn't appear on the spectrum above, but it is a tactic most often practised by monopolistic firms.

At the end of the Oligopoly chapter (Chapter 12) you will find a guide to helping you draw the market structure diagrams (see pages 84–5).

- Definition of a market structure
- Brief introduction to each market structure and their relationship to one another
- How the market structure chapters will be organised

8 Perfect Competition

aims
- To outline the characteristics of perfect competition
- To describe the short run equilibrium of a firm in perfect competition
- To explain the transition to the long run
- To identify advantages and disadvantages of perfect competition

Characteristics of perfect competition

- **No barriers to entry**. Firms can enter and leave the industry as and when they choose. Existing firms cannot prevent new firms from entering.
- A **large number of buyers and sellers**, each of which controls too little market share to influence market price.
- A **high degree of knowledge**. Every firm, and every potential entrant, knows the profit and cost levels of every other firm. Consumers have knowledge of who is charging the lowest price.
- **Homogenous products**. All firms sell identical products, making competitive advertising pointless (since you end up advertising your competitors' products as well as your own) and meaning that there is no brand loyalty.

- A **perfectly elastic supply of the factors of production**, i.e. the cost per unit remains the same.
- All firms aim to **maximise profits**. This happens, as we already know, when MC = MR.

Clearly, perfect competition is highly unrealistic. Try setting up an airline and you'll quickly discover what barriers to entry are. Search for two competing brands of car or lipstick or candle that are so identical you cannot tell the difference between them, and you'll quickly see that there is nearly always a difference, however small. Try listing the exact price of petrol at every service station in Ireland and you'll quickly see that a high degree of knowledge doesn't exist either.

exam focus

So why study something if it's never going to happen? We study it because it's an ideal, i.e. it would be better for consumers if there were fewer barriers to entry, it would be better if there were more firms competing for our loyalty, and it would be better if we had more information. Perfect competition could be considered the economic equivalent of world peace. World peace doesn't exist either and never has, but it's also an ideal we can aim for, and against which we can measure the real world. So we can sometimes learn more about what actually happens by imagining something that doesn't happen.

Short run

- In perfect competition, because there is freedom of entry, and all goods are homogenous, each firm is too small to influence the market price.
- If one firm charged more than the other firms, it would sell nothing and go out of business. If it charged less, all other firms would lower their price to match it.
- Therefore, each firm is a **price taker**: they have no choice but to charge the same as everyone else – the market price.
- This results in a flat average revenue (AR) (demand) curve, and a flat marginal revenue (MR) curve.
- The firm faces a U-shaped average cost (AC) curve with the marginal cost (MC) curve cutting it upward at its lowest point.
- The equilibrium is derived by:
  - Finding the profit-maximising position at MC = MR (circled in red).
  - Drawing a line straight down to find the quantity (Q_1).
  - Going across to the price axis to find the price (P_1).
  - The profit made on each unit sold is the difference between average revenue (AR) and average cost (AC). When this is multiplied by the quantity sold, it tells us the supernormal profit the firm earns (the red rectangle P_1-b-c-d).
$$SNP = Q(AR - AC)$$
  - The firm is wasteful of resources, since its average cost per unit (point d) does not correspond with the lowest point on the AC curve.

- The section of the MC curve that lies above the average variable cost (AVC) curve is effectively also the **Short Run Supply Curve** of the firm, i.e. it tells you what quantity the firm would be willing to supply at each price, since MC = MR must occur somewhere along it. The lowest point on the

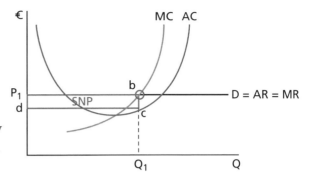

average variable cost curve represents the lowest price the firm can charge and still stay in business in the short run. Therefore, the section of the MC curve that lies below the AVC curve doesn't form part of the short run supply curve.

Transition from short run to long run

In the long run (LR), when all factors have changed:

- New firms enter the market due to a combination of three factors:
  - Supernormal profit was earned in the short run (SR).
  - Due to perfect knowledge, the new firms know about this.
  - There are no barriers to entry.
- The arrival of new firms causes the *industry* supply curve to shift to the right, forcing the price down from P_1 to P_2.
- Since each firm is a price taker, this forces each firm's price – and AR/MR curve – downward:
  - If it falls below the lowest point on the AC curve, the firm goes out of business.
  - For those that survive, it cuts the lowest point on the AC curve exactly, meaning that in the long run the only profit anyone earns is normal profit.
    MC = MR = AC = AR
    $$SNP = Q(AR - AC)$$
  - If supernormal profit is ever earned again, new firms immediately enter the market and the process is repeated.

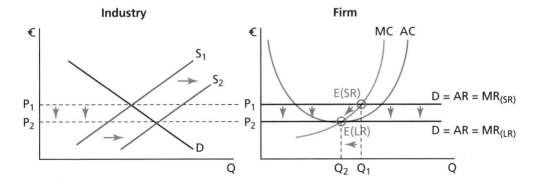

So that we arrive at a long run equilibrium that looks like this:

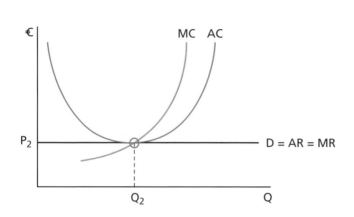

As with the other chapters on market structures, thinking your way through the step-by-step explanation is much better than trying to memorise without understanding. Remember: everything in the diagrams is based on the characteristics.

Advantages of perfect competition

- The consumer gets the good for the lowest possible price that still allows the seller to remain in business, and therefore the consumer is not exploited.
- There is no waste of resources, such as on persuasive and competitive advertising.
- Efficiency is encouraged, since anyone who cannot produce at the lowest point on the AC goes out of business.

Disadvantages of perfect competition

- Goods are homogenous, so consumers don't get any variety.
- Firms are constantly only one step away from going out of business. This may discourage entrepreneurship, since entrepreneurs like to have some security and certainty in exchange for their risk-taking.
- No SNP to invest in research and development.
- Each firm has only a small market share, and so may not benefit from economies of scale. As a result, AC may be higher than if there were fewer, larger firms. That would be of little benefit to the consumer however, since the price would also be higher due to less competition.

Don't forget that whether something is 'good' or 'bad' in Economics depends on whose point of view you're looking from. Firms hate perfect competition because they make only normal profit in the LR, and love monopoly since they don't have to worry about competition. On the other side of the counter, consumers want low prices or variety or both, and hence prefer perfect or imperfect competition. The most common outcome – in Ireland at least – often seems to be oligopoly.

key point

- Characteristics of perfect competition
- Short run equilibrium in perfect competition
- Transition to the long run equilibrium
- Advantages and disadvantages of perfect competition

exam Q

2016, Section A, Question 1

The diagram below shows a firm operating under conditions of perfect competition in the short run.

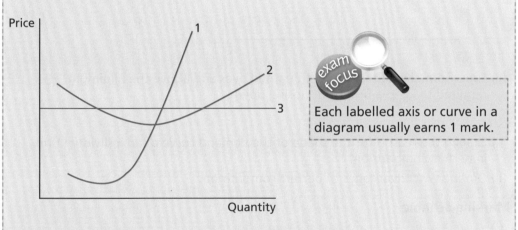

exam focus

Each labelled axis or curve in a diagram usually earns 1 mark.

(a) What is represented by the lines numbered 1 and 3?

(b)

    (i) Show clearly on the diagram the total supernormal profits of the firm.

    (ii) Explain the term supernormal profit.

Marking scheme

- 3 correctly labelled lines @ 3 marks each
- 3 marks for showing supernormal profits
- 4 marks for defining supernormal profits
- 16 marks in total

exam focus

Try to keep your explanation as simple as you can. Imagine that you are explaining the diagram to someone who never saw it before. Tell them step-by-step why each line is shaped like it is, and why the firm does what it does.

Answer

Number	Name
1	Marginal Cost
2	Average Cost
3	Average Revenue/Marginal Revenue/Demand

(i)

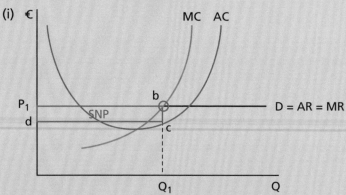

(ii) Supernormal profit is any profit earned over and above the minimum required to keep a firm from closing down.

2012, Section B, Question 2 (a)

(i) Explain the reason for the shape of the demand curve of an individual firm in perfect competition.

(ii) Outline two advantages of perfect competition.

Marking scheme

(i)

- 2 reasons @ 6 marks and 4 marks

(ii)

- 2 advantages @ 5 marks each
- 20 marks in total

Answer

(i)

- In a perfectly competitive market, each firm is a price taker and must adopt the market price, the 'going rate'.
- Since each firm produces such a small fraction of the overall output, it has no influence on market price.
- Since each firm sells identical products, any increase in price will cause consumers to switch to cheaper competitors.

(ii)

- **Consumers not exploited:** Due to freedom of entry, the SNP earned in the SR attract new entrants, resulting in normal profit in the LR.
- **Efficiency:** The firm operates at the lowest point on the average costs curve, meaning that there is no waste of resources.
- **Low consumer prices:** The firms sells at the lowest possible price to allow it to remain in business.
- **No competitive advertising:** Since goods are homogeneous there is no need for competitive advertising, which would necessitate higher prices to cover its cost.

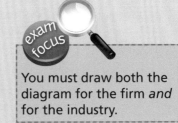

You must draw both the diagram for the firm *and* for the industry.

2012, Section B, Question 2 (b)

(i) Explain, with the aid of a labelled diagram, the equilibrium position of a firm in short run perfect competition.

(ii) With the aid of labelled diagrams, explain the impact which the entry of new firms would have on the market and on the equilibrium position of the firm.

Marking scheme

(i)

- 7 marks for the diagram.
- 10 marks for the explanation (5 points @ 2 marks each)

(ii)

- 4 marks for the market diagram
- 4 marks for the firm diagram
- 10 marks for the explanation (5 points @ 2 marks each)
- 35 marks in total

Each labelled axis or curve in a diagram usually earns 1 mark.

Answer

(i) In the SR, the perfectly competitive firm faces:

- A U-shaped AC curve with the MC curve cutting it upward at its lowest point.
- Flat AR and AC curves, since it's a price taker.
- It maximises profit at MC = MR (circled).
- The profit on each unit sold is AR − AC. When this is multiplied by Q, it tells you the supernormal profit earned.
- In the SR, the firm makes supernormal profit.

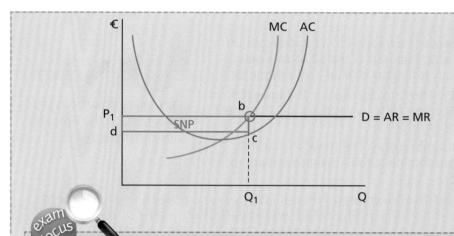

exam focus

Try to keep your explanation as simple as you can. Imagine that you are explaining the diagram to someone who never saw it before. Tell them step-by-step why each line is shaped like it is, and why the firm does what it does.

(ii)

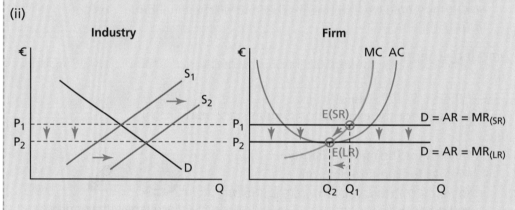

- In the LR, new firms enter the industry because:
  - There are no barriers to entry.
  - They want to take some of the supernormal profit that was earned in the SR.
  - Since there is perfect knowledge, they know about this supernormal profit.

exam focus

You must draw both the diagram for the firm *and* for the industry.

- Their entry causes the market supply curve to shift to the right.
- This drives down the market price from P1 to P2. Since each firm is a price taker, it must now charge P2.
- The firm still maximises profits at MC = MR. Any firms that don't go out of business will be forced to charge a price that is at the lowest point on the AC curve.
- Therefore, since AR = AC for each unit sold, the firm only makes normal profit in the LR.

9 Monopoly

aims
- To outline the characteristics of monopoly
- To describe the short run equilibrium of a firm in monopoly
- To explain the transition to the long run
- To compare monopoly with perfect competition
- To identify advantages and disadvantages of monopoly

Characteristics of monopoly

- **Barriers to entry**. It is impossible for other firms to set up in competition with the monopolist.
- **Only one firm**. The firm and the industry are one and the same thing. As a result, there is no competition.
- **A high degree of knowledge**. Everyone knows the profit and cost levels experienced by the monopolist, but due to the barriers to entry they are unable to take advantage of their knowledge.
- The firm aims to **maximise profits**. The monopolist maximises their profit at MC = MR.

Where do monopolies come from?

- **Legal monopoly**: The government may give a firm the sole right to run a particular type of business, e.g. the company that operates the Luas. Usually a licence is issued for a number of years, and must be competed for again when that period ends.

- **Natural monopoly**: Sometimes it is not possible to survive in business unless you have all or nearly all of the market, e.g. it would not make financial sense to have a second rail line from Dublin to Galway, making Iarnrod Éireann a 'natural' monopolist on this line.
- **Copyrights or patents**: These are legal mechanisms by which the inventor of a product or the writer of a book can legally prevent anyone else from selling it for a set number of years. It is intended to encourage entrepreneurship, by giving inventors a greater chance of making money.
- **Economies of scale**: The larger a firm gets, generally the lower its average cost (AC) becomes. This can act as a barrier to small firms, since they cannot compete on price.
- **Mergers and takeovers**: Monopolies have sometimes arisen because a large firm manages to buy all the smaller ones. Because it reduces competition, governments usually require large firms to seek government permission before merging or taking each other over.
- **Access to a raw material**: If a firm has sole access to an important raw material, and doesn't sell it to anyone else, it can gain a monopoly position, e.g. an oil drilling company.
- **Product differentiation**: Through advertising and branding, a firm can build up consumer loyalty – particularly if it is based on genuine quality rather than just image. If a business is like an economic 'castle' with an unbreachable 'moat', the more likely it is to stand the test of time due to its enduring competitive advantage, e.g. Coca-Cola.
- **Brand proliferation**: When existing firms flood the market with a range of brands, putting pressure on new entrants to offer a similarly wide range.
- **Trade agreements**: Sometimes competing firms agree to divide up the market by region, making each of them a monopolist in their own area (see Chapter 12).

Short run

- Since the firm and the industry are one and the same, the firm's demand curve is the industry demand curve, i.e. a downward-sloping average revenue (AR) curve. This means that a firm in monopoly can decide price or quantity but not both:
  - If it chooses a price, the consumers will decide how much they will buy at that price.
  - If it sets a particular quantity, the consumers will effectively decide what price will be paid.
- The monopolist faces a U-shaped AC curve with the MC cutting it upward at its lowest point.

- The equilibrium is derived by:
  - Finding the profit-maximising position at MC = MR (circled in red).
  - Drawing a line straight down to find the quantity (Q_1)
  - Tracing a line up to the AR curve and then across to the price axis to find the price (P_1).
  - The profit on each unit sold is AR − AC. When this is multiplied by Q, it gives the supernormal profit earned (P_1-b-c-d).

    $$SNP = Q(AR - AC)$$

  - The firm's average cost of production is d. Since it is not at the lowest point on the AC curve, the firm is wasteful of resources.

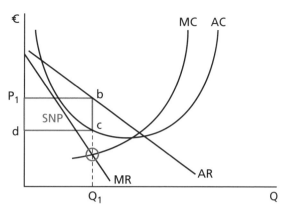

Again, don't just try to memorise. Work your way through the explanation while keeping in mind what the monopolist is trying to achieve. Remember: the diagrams are based solely on the characteristics.

Transition from short run to long run

In the long run, since there are barriers to entry, no new firms are able to enter the market. As a result, the monopolist continues to exploit the consumer by making supernormal profits, and continues to be wasteful of resources.

Comparison of monopoly with perfect competition

When comparing monopoly with perfect competition, it is best to superimpose one diagram on the other. Here we see monopoly depicted in green and perfect competition depicted in blue. The AC and MC curves are in black since they are common to both. We see the following differences:

- While a perfectly competitive firm charged a price at the lowest point on the AC curve (P_{PC}), the monopolist charged a much higher price (P_M). Thus the perfectly competitive firm is more efficient.
- The perfectly competitive firm makes normal profits in the LR, while the monopolist enjoys supernormal profits. Thus we can say that the monopolist is 'exploiting' the consumer.

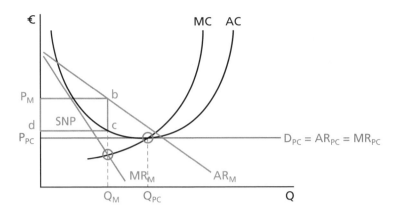

Advantages of monopoly

- **Economies of scale**: Since there is only one firm, it has the chance to reduce its AC much lower than a larger number of smaller firms could do. Of course, this benefits the consumer only if it results in a lower price, which may be unlikely.
- **Monopolies last longer**, giving their employees greater job security, their shareholders greater certainty and their customers greater reassurance through after-sales service.
- **Monopolies avoid duplication**, e.g. competition in the bus market can lead to congestion, resulting in a social cost to consumers.
- **Less advertising**: Monopolies don't have to engage in competitive advertising. However, this is good for the consumer only if the savings result in lower prices.

Disadvantages of monopoly

- **Consumers are exploited**: With no competition to worry about, the firm can charge a higher price than the minimum it needs to in order to stay in business.
- **No choice or variety**: If you want the product, there is only one producer you can buy it from. Whatever their terms and conditions, standard of service or level of quality, you have to put up with it or do without.
- **Waste of resources**: The monopolist doesn't operate at the lowest point on the AC curve.
- There is the potential for **Price discrimination** (see Chapter 10).
- **Less innovation**: If you have the market to yourself, you don't have to bother coming up with new ideas in order to survive. This is bad for consumers. It can be argued that it is also bad for firms, and that they should welcome competition because it keeps them on their toes.
- **Inefficiency**: Since there is no competition, firms don't do their best to keep down costs, resulting in higher prices for consumers.

Because the disadvantages of monopoly for society are considered to outweigh the advantages, the government tries to break up monopolies and/or introduce competition, even in the case of monopolies it set up itself when it was the only entity in a position to do so, e.g. ESB.

The last part of a Section B question will frequently ask you what you would do if you were the government, e.g. how you would deal with a monopolistic firm.

key point

- Characteristics of monopoly
- Short run equilibrium of a firm in monopoly
- Transition to the long run equilibrium
- Comparison between monopoly and perfect competition
- Advantages and disadvantages of monopoly

exam Q

2015, Section B, Question 2 (a)

(i) State and explain two examples of barriers to entry facing firms wishing to enter a monopoly market.
(ii) Explain, with the aid of a diagram, the long run equilibrium position of a monopolist. Identify on your diagram the profit the monopolist makes.

Marking scheme
- 2 barriers @ 5 marks each
- 11 marks for diagram @ 1 mark each
- 14 marks for explanation
- 35 marks in total

Answer

(i)
- **Natural monopoly:** It may not be possible to survive unless you have a very high market share.
- **Legal monopoly:** A firm may have the sole legal right to operate in an industry.
- **Access to raw materials:** A firm may own all of a vital raw material.
- **Mergers and takeovers:** One firm may succeed in buying all of its competitors.
- **Economies of scale:** As a firm grows, usually its AC falls.
- **Copyrights:** These allow a writer to prevent others from copying their work.
- **Product proliferation and differentiation:** A firm creates a range of products that attract high customer loyalty.

- **Collusion:** This is when competing firms divide up the market between them, making each of them a monopolist in their local region.

(ii)

- The firm faces downward sloping AR and MR curves, since it can dictate P or Q but not both.

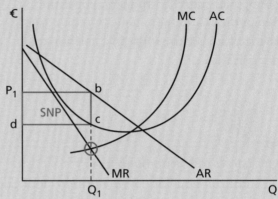

- It has a U-shaped AC curve with the MC curve cutting it upward at its lowest point.

- Profit is maximised at MC = MR (circled), where MC is rising. The firm therefore sells Q1 and charges price P1.

- Since there are barriers to entry, in the long run, AR is still greater than AC for each unit sold.

- As a result, the monopolist in the LR still earns supernormal profit (P1-b-c-d).

- Since the firm does not operate at the lowest point on the AC curve, there is a waste of resources. The cost of production is shown at point d.

2013, Section B, Question 2 (a)

(ii) Outline two reasons why monopolies may not be in the public interest.

Marking scheme

- 2 reasons @ 5 marks each
- 10 marks in total

Answer

- **Super Normal Profits:** If a monopolist charges a price above AC then it will earn SNPs at the expense of the consumer.

- **Inefficient:** Monopolies not producing at the lowest point of the AC curve results in waste of scarce resources.

- **Higher Prices:** Monopolies can charge higher prices, compared to perfect competition, because there is no competition.

- **Lower output:** A monopolist with similar costs to a perfectly competitive firm is likely to produce at a lower quantity.

- **Lower quality and less innovation:** Since monopolies have no competition, they have less reason either to maintain high quality or to develop new products.

- **Price discrimination:** Monopolies may have the ability to charge different consumers different prices for the same product, thereby increasing their supernormal profits (see Chapter 10).

- **Burden on the taxpayer:** Any losses made by state-owned monopolies such as Iarnrod Éireann must be borne by the taxpayer.

10 Price Discrimination

aims
- To define price discrimination
- To outline the three different types
- To set out the conditions necessary to practise price discrimination
- To discuss some additional conditions that make it easier to practise
- To show how price discrimination works in action

Introduction

Price Discrimination refers to the practice of charging different consumers two different prices for the very same product or service **where the difference in price is not due to a difference in cost**.

There are three different types:

- **1st degree price discrimination**: The seller tries to eliminate consumer surplus by charging each consumer the maximum they would be willing to pay. In reality this is rarely achieved, given the difficulty of finding out the maximum price each consumer has in mind.

- **2nd degree price discrimination**: Larger quantities are sold at a lower average price, i.e. the consumer can save by bulk-buying, even though each unit costs the same to make.

BUY ONE GET ONE FREE

exam focus

If every consumer who walked in the door had their maximum price stamped on their forehead, 1st degree price discrimination might just be possible. Since they usually don't, 3rd degree price discrimination is the next best thing.

- **3rd degree price discrimination**: The seller charges different groups different prices, based on location, age, income, etc., e.g. charging students a lower price for gym membership than adults. A seller cannot eliminate all consumer surplus, but this eliminates a lot of it.

Conditions for price discrimination

In order to practise price discrimination, there are three necessary conditions (if you don't have some or all of these, you cannot practise price discrimination):

- Some **monopoly power**. If there is freedom of entry into the market in which the higher price is being charged, it becomes impossible to charge two different prices.

- **Distinct and separate markets.** It shouldn't be possible for anyone to buy in the cheaper market and sell in the dearer one. This is called **arbitrage.** If it happened, it would quickly cause the price difference to disappear.
- Different **price elasticities of demand.** Consumers in each market must have a different tolerance for price increases.

There are also some additional conditions (you don't *need* these conditions, but having them helps you to practise price discrimination):

- **Brand loyalty.** When a consumer finds a brand they like, or that's reliable, they tend to stick with it. Researching products takes time and effort. As a result, they may be willing to pay a higher price, e.g. always buying a Toyota car. Additionally, sellers try to inspire loyalty for the purpose of charging higher prices.
- **Consumer ignorance.** Up until now, we've assumed a high degree of knowledge. In the real world, consumers aren't always aware that a good can be bought for less somewhere else, e.g. cheaper dental treatment abroad.
- **Consumer inertia.** Even if they are aware that a good is cheaper elsewhere, the difference in price isn't always large enough to go to the trouble of switching, e.g. not bothering to shop around when renewing car or health insurance.

Price discrimination in action

Imagine a firm operating in two markets, one under conditions of perfect competition (blue), the other under conditions of monopoly (green):

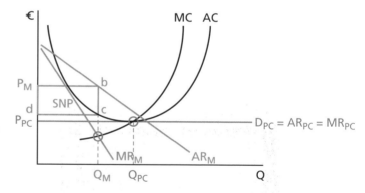

In order to maximise profit, the firm does not charge each market the same price. Instead:

- It charges P_1 in the monopolistic market and makes supernormal profits. Charging a lower price would yield less profit.
- It charges P_2 in the perfectly competitive market and makes normal profits. Charging a higher price would yield less profit.

Note that there is only one set of cost curves in the diagram, indicating that the cost is the same in each market. This is in keeping with the definition of price discrimination.

Also, keep in mind that the two markets don't have to be perfect competition and monopoly. They could be two different monopoly markets, for example. As long as there are different elasticities (i.e. different slopes on the two AR curves), there is scope for price discrimination.

key point

- Definition of price discrimination
- Three different types of price discrimination
- Conditions necessary to practise price discrimination
- Additional conditions that make it easier to practise
- Price discrimination in action

exam Q

2015, Section B, Question 2 (b)
A monopolist can increase its profits by engaging in price discrimination.
 (i) Explain the concept of price discrimination, using a suitable example.
(ii) State and explain the market conditions necessary for price discrimination to take place.

Marking scheme
 (i) ● Definition of price discrimination @ 8 marks
     ● Example @ 2 marks
(ii)
     ● 3 conditions @ 5 marks (2 for stating, 3 for explaining)
     ● 25 marks in total

Answer
 (i)
     ● Price discrimination involves charging two different consumers two different prices for the very same product or service where the difference in price is not due to a difference in cost. The aim of the seller is to eliminate consumer surplus.
     Possible examples:
     ● Peak and off-peak commuter ticket prices
     ● Adult and student prices for cinema tickets
     ● Three bottles of shampoo for the price of two
(ii)
     ● **Some monopoly power:** New firms must be prevented from entering the market in which the higher price is being charged – otherwise there couldn't be two prices.
     ● **Separation of markets:** It must be impossible to buy in the cheap market and sell in the dear market. Otherwise, the price difference would quickly disappear.
     ● **Different consumer price elasticities of demand:** Consumers with a greater need for the product or a greater ability to pay are charged higher prices. More price sensitive consumers are charged less. If all consumers had the same PED, price discrimination would be impossible.

- To outline the characteristics of imperfect competition
- To describe the short run equilibrium of a firm in imperfect competition
- To explain the transition to the long run
- To compare imperfect competition with perfect competition
- To identify advantages and disadvantages of imperfect competition

Characteristics of imperfect competition

- **No barriers to entry**. Firms can enter and leave the industry as and when they choose. Existing firms cannot prevent new firms from entering.
- A **large number of sellers**, each of which is too small to influence market price.
- A **large number of buyers**, each of which is too small to influence market price.
- A **high degree of knowledge**. Every firm, and every potential entrant, knows the profit and cost levels of every other firm. Consumers have knowledge of who is charging the lowest price.
- **Differentiated products**. All firms sell similar but not identical products, meaning that it makes sense for firms to spend money on competitive advertising and on making their products unique.
- All firms aim to **maximise profits**. This happens, as we already know, when MC = MR.

Short run

- Since each firm is selling a unique product, it has some degree of monopoly power. This results in a downward-sloping AR curve, much like in monopoly.
- The imperfectly competitive firm faces a U-shaped AC curve with the MC cutting it upward at its lowest point.
- The equilibrium is derived by:
  - Finding the profit-maximising position at MC = MR (circled in red).
  - Drawing a line straight down to find the quantity (Q_1)
  - Tracing a line up to the AR curve and then across to the price axis to find the price (P_1).
  - The profit on each unit sold is AR − AC. When this is multiplied by Q, it gives the supernormal profit earned (P_1-b-c-d).
    $$\text{SNP} = Q(\text{AR} - \text{AC})$$
  - Since the average cost of production (point d) is above the lowest price on the AC curve, the firm is wasteful of resources.

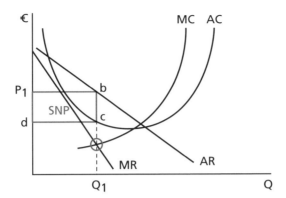

Transition from short run to long run

- In the LR, much like in perfect competition, new firms enter the industry because:
  - Supernormal profits were earned in the short run.
  - Due to the assumption of a high degree of knowledge, this was widely known.
  - There are no barriers to entry.
- The entry of these new firms causes the industry supply curve to shift to the right, in turn causing the price to drop as firms compete for customers.

Since the firms sell differentiated products, they are not price takers. However, as new firms enter the market, competition still forces the average price downward.

- Each firm now has a smaller share of the market, so the individual firm's AR curve shifts to the left until such time as it is tangential to the AC curve.
- In the LR, only normal profits are being made at the profit maximising position of MC = MR (circled in red). Therefore, AR = AC.

$$SNP = Q(AR - AC)$$

- As in the SR, the firm is wasteful of resources since it is not operating at the lowest point on the AC curve.
- Any firms that cannot make a normal profit (whose AR curve shifts further to the left than the AC curve) go out of business.

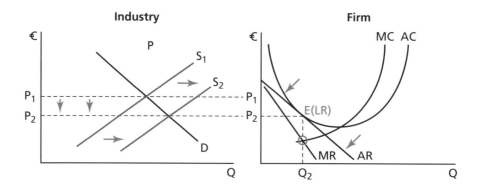

Comparison of perfect competition with imperfect competition

As we have already done with monopoly, we can now compare perfect competition with imperfect competition:

Work your way through the explanation while asking yourself, What would I do if I were this firm? Remember: the diagrams are not 'separate' from the characteristics – they're based on them.

- As we can see in the diagram below, the imperfectly competitive firm (green) is wasteful of resources since the price it charges (P_{IMC}) is not at the lowest point on the AC curve. This is due to the costs of persuasive advertising and product differentiation, costs which are not incurred in perfect competition (blue).

- However, things are not as bad for the consumer as they were in a monopoly, since the imperfectly competitive firm does not make supernormal profits in the LR.

- On the other hand, imperfect competition offers something of value to consumers that perfect competition does not: variety. Most people are happy for sticky tape or paper clips to be homogenous, but would not like all breakfast cereals or wristwatches to be identical – even if it made them cheaper. We like variety, and most of us are willing to pay a little for it. Therefore, despite the higher price, imperfect competition may be the more attractive of the two in many instances.

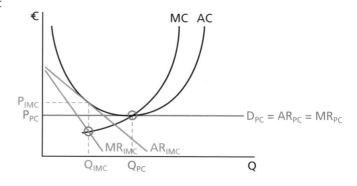

Advantages of imperfect competition

- Consumers are not exploited in the LR, since the firm earns only normal profits. The consumer has only to pay only the minimum required to keep the firm in business.

- It offers the consumer choice and variety. Goods are similar but not identical, e.g. after-sales service may be better than in perfect competition.
- It creates employment in the advertising industry. Persuasive advertising, however, except perhaps for entertainment value, doesn't benefit consumers. If anything, it may impose a social cost, e.g. junk mail.
- In turn, advertising is good for sports teams in terms of sponsorship, newspaper costs are reduced due to advertising, etc.

Disadvantage of imperfect competition

- Waste of resources: firms don't operate at the lowest point on the AC curve. This is accounted for by the cost of advertising and any cost incurred in making products unique, costs that are passed on to the consumer.

- Characteristics of imperfect competition
- Short run equilibrium of a firm in imperfect competition
- Transition to the long run equilibrium
- Comparison between imperfect and perfect competition
- Advantages and disadvantages of imperfect competition

2014, Section B, Question 2 (a)

(i) State and explain three assumptions underlying the theory of imperfect competition.

(ii) Explain why a firm's demand curve under imperfect competition differs from a firm's demand curve under perfect competition.

Marking scheme
- 3 assumptions @ 5 marks, 4 marks and 4 marks
- 2 points of explanation @ 6 marks each
- 25 marks in total

Answer
(i)

- No barriers to entry or exit. Firms are free to enter or leave the industry as and when they wish.
- A large number of buyers and sellers, each of which is too small to influence market price.
- A high degree of knowledge among competing firms, potential entrants and consumers.

- Product differentiation. Firms sell similar but not identical products, and make use of persuasive advertising to attract consumers.
- Firms aim to maximise profits at the point where MC = MR.

(ii)

- **Perfect competition:** Because each firm is selling an homogeneous product and controls so little of the market, any price increase will cause all consumers to switch to a cheaper competitor. This makes the firm a price taker. The demand curve is perfectly elastic and therefore horizontal.
- **Imperfect competition:** Because each firm is selling a differentiated or unique product, there is scope for some degree of brand loyalty. A price increase will not cause all consumers to switch to a cheaper competitor. Demand is no longer perfectly elastic and the demand curve is therefore downward-sloping.

2014, Section B, Question 2 (b)

(i) Explain, with the aid of a diagram, the long run equilibrium of a firm in imperfect competition.

(ii) With reference to your diagram in (b) (i) explain why the firm is not making socially efficient use of scarce resources.

Marking scheme

- Diagram @ 10 marks
- Explanation @ 8 marks
- 3 points of explanation @ 4 marks each
- 30 marks in total

Answer

(i)

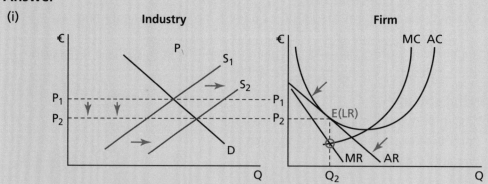

- In the LR, new firms enter the industry, causing the industry supply curve to shift to the right, and in turn causing the market price to fall to P2.
- The firm's AR curve shifts to the left until such time as it is tangential to the AC curve at point E.
- Profit is still maximized at MC = MR (circled in red), but because now AR = AC, only normal profit is now earned.

- The price is not at the lowest point on the AC curve, meaning there is a waste of resources.

(ii)

- The firm is not making socially efficient use of scarce resources due the cost of both product differentiation and persuasive advertising.
- These costs are passed on to the consumer in the form of higher prices, meaning that the firm does not operate at the lowest point on the AC curve, meaning that the firm has capacity left unused.
- The consumer gains product variety at the cost of society inefficiency.

2013 Section B, Question 2 (c)

The global market for toothpaste products can be described as an imperfectly competitive market, where firms engage in competitive advertising and branding.

(i) Explain the term 'competitive advertising'.

(ii) Outline, using an example, how advertising can be used to prevent small firms entering an industry.

(iii) State and explain two possible disadvantages of advertising for the consumer.

Marking scheme

(i)

- Definition of competitive advertising @ 7 marks

(ii)

- Explanation @ 3 marks
- Example @ 3 marks

(iii)

- 2 disadvantages @ 6 marks each
- 25 marks in total

Answer

(i)

Competitive advertising attempts to favourably compare a product or service with its competitors, highlighting differences in the minds of consumers, e.g. a brand of batteries which it is claimed lasts 50% longer than the best rival brand.

(ii)

An existing large firm may launch an expensive advertising campaigns that newer, smaller entrants could find prohibitively costly. This constitutes a barrier to entry.

Example: A large airline launches an expensive TV ad campaign to keep a potential entrant from entering the market.

(iii)

- **Higher prices:** The costs of advertising are passed on to consumers in the form of higher prices.
- **Nuisance:** Whether in the form of junk mail, increased litter, unsightly billboards or unwanted TV ad breaks, advertising can be a source of annoyance for consumers.

- **Information overload:** While variety is a good thing, consumers may not have time to examine the many complicated alternatives they are presented with, e.g. phone plans.

- **Impulse buying:** Advertising can cause consumers to buy products on the spur of the moment, therefore wasting some of their limited incomes.

- **Misleading or false ads:** Advertisements can make exaggerated or false claims regarding products or services.

- **Unrealistic expectations:** Through advertising on the basis of image, impressionable consumers may be persuaded to pursue a lifestyle which is unattainable, e.g. buying a product because a famous actor or singer claims to use it.

- **Harmful goods:** Without careful regulation, advertising can increase the sale of harmful products such as cigarettes or alcohol.

12 Oligopoly

Characteristics of oligopoly

- **Barriers to entry** exist. It is difficult for new firms to enter the market, and the firms already in the market make it as hard as possible for them to do so.
- **A few large firms**, who between them make up all or nearly all of the output in the industry. This is also described as a **high concentration ratio**.
- **Product differentiation**. As in imperfect competition, firms sell similar but not identical products.
- **Firms are interdependent**. Because there are only a few firms, each is capable of influencing market price. Each time a firm considers a change in price, they take into account the possible reaction of competitors, much like a game of rock-paper-scissors.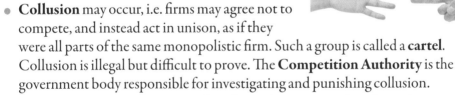
- **Collusion** may occur, i.e. firms may agree not to compete, and instead act in unison, as if they were all parts of the same monopolistic firm. Such a group is called a **cartel**. Collusion is illegal but difficult to prove. The **Competition Authority** is the government body responsible for investigating and punishing collusion.
- A **high degree of knowledge** of profits and costs exists, but due to barriers to entry, this knowledge is of limited value.
- Firms usually aim to **maximise profits**. Once again, this happens at MC = MR.

exam focus

This is the most realistic of the market structures, certainly in Ireland but also internationally. From mobile phones to banking, supermarkets and insurance, again and again we find industries dominated by a small number of large producers.

Firms in an oligopolistic industry face downward-sloping but (according to economist Paul Sweezy) 'kinked' AR and MR curves.

The AR is kinked due to **Price Rigidity.** This refers to the reluctance of rival firms to raise prices even if they experience small cost increases and vice versa.

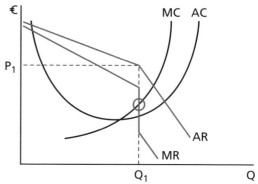

- Raising price above P_1 is bad because if the other firms keep their prices the same, you lose customers and therefore profit. You could hope that they'd increase their prices along with yours, resulting in more revenue for everyone, but you cannot trust them to do so (since they have an incentive not to do so). This part of the AR curve is relatively elastic – a 1% increase in price causes a greater than 1% fall in quantity demanded.

- Lowering price below P_1 is also bad because you have no choice but to assume that the other firms will follow suit, resulting in lower revenue for everyone. As a result, there's no point in lowering price. This part of the AR curve is relatively inelastic – a 1% drop in price causes a less than 1% increase in quantity demanded.

- Either way, you lose revenue. This phenomenon is also called 'sticky prices'. The graph doesn't explain very well how that price was arrived at in the first place, but once it is arrived at, it explains very well why there is a tendency for it not to change.

- Since firms do not wish to change their prices, **non-price competition** is common, i.e. competing on the basis of sponsorship, free gifts or especially advertising.

The MR curve is also kinked, but for a different reason. **Price Constancy** refers to the reluctance of a firm in oligopoly to change prices because the cost of doing so exceeds the potential gain in profit, e.g. the cost of printing new fliers and placing new advertisements may be more than the extra revenue gained from changing the price. As a result, in the diagram below, when the MR curve rises by a small amount, the new profit-maximising position ($MC_2 = MR$) results in the exact same price and quantity as the old equilibrium position ($MC_1 = MR$). This is why the MR curve contains a vertical section.

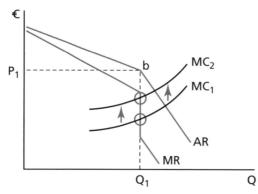

exam focus

Don't confuse price rigidity and price constancy. They both refer to a reluctance to change price, but for different reasons.

The firm maximises its profits at $MC = MR$. Because there are barriers to entry, the firm exploits the consumer by making supernormal profit in both the SR and the LR. It is also wasteful of resources since it does not operate at the lowest point on the AC curve.

$$SNP = Q(AR - AC)$$

A special feature of oligopoly is **collusion**. Since there are only a few producers, it is easier for them to conspire together than it would be for the many firms in a perfectly or imperfectly competitive market to do so. Types of collusion include:

- Agreeing to charge a common higher price, e.g. all filling stations in a town agree to increase petrol prices by 20%.
- Agreeing to restrict output, forcing consumers to outbid each other, e.g. oil-producing countries agree to lower production, forcing up its price.

- Agreeing to temporarily drop prices to keep a potential new entrant out of the market, e.g. mobile phone companies operate at a loss to persuade a new entrant to stay out.
- Dividing up the country between different firms, giving each a monopoly position in their designated area, e.g. one firm will serve the north-side of Dublin, another will serve the south-side.
- Giving different market segments to different firms, again making each a monopolist in their segment, e.g. home insurance and car insurance.

The problem with collusion is that once all firms raise their price, each individual one then has an incentive to 'cheat' by lowering theirs again, in order to steal market share from the others. Of course, the others quickly follow. When all firms' prices have been lowered, the incentive returns to make **another** agreement, which is followed by more cheating. Such a cycle can eventually settle at a price that *on average* is lower than in monopoly but higher than in perfect competition.

When firms charge similar prices, this is not in and of itself evidence of collusion, which must involve a direct agreement. It may instead be caused by **price leadership**, which occurs when the market is dominated by a large supplier whose smaller competitors have little choice but to copy. There is little point in risking a price war with a larger firm that has the economies of scale to lower prices much lower than you can. A safer option is simply to charge the price they charge.

Objectives other than profit-maximisation

We have assumed until now that firms aim to maximise profit, but there may be occasions not only in oligopoly but in all market structures when firms may not wish to do so:

- Large supernormal profits attract the attention of the government, which may try to bring more competition into the market, which can result in lower profits in the LR.

- A business owner may not be willing to spend the time and energy needed to expand their business, especially if they are already financially secure or are nearing retirement. Leisure activities may take priority.

- Expanding a business will often mean taking on extra debt, or having to share control of the business with others.

- On the other hand, a firm that *does* wish to expand may choose to lower its price and suffer temporary losses in order to gain market share.

- A firm may engage in limit pricing to keep a potential entrant out of the market, temporarily lowering profit in the process.

- Bonuses for managers are often based on maximising **revenue**, not profit, e.g. a bank manager issuing as many mortgages as possible, regardless of the long-term effect on profit. This is called the **principal-agent problem**: the interests of employees can be different to those of the firm they work for.

This is a good example of how there are exceptions to all Economic laws. People are not robots. Each person is different. They are subject to many competing objectives, and so don't always behave as some textbook might predict.

Drawing the diagrams

Now that we have looked at all of the market structures, it's a good time to develop a system for drawing the various diagrams.

Many students are put off by the diagrams in these chapters, and indeed by the diagrams across the course in general. The simplest way of dealing with this problem is by tackling it head-on – think your way through the explanation step by step, don't study a chapter unless you have already studied material in it that was explained in a previous chapter, and then practise, practise, practise until you know them by heart and understand them thoroughly.

When practising your market structure diagrams, follow the step-by-step **ACRES** rule:

- First draw your **Axes**, making sure to label them (P, Q, etc.). Without a label, an axis isn't an axis, it's just a line.

- Second, draw your **Cost curves**. The AC curve is U-shaped, and the MC curve cuts it upward at its lowest point.

- Third, draw the **Revenue** curves. For perfect competition, these will be horizontal. For monopoly and imperfect competition, they will be downward-sloping. For oligopoly, they will be kinked. Beware of any differences in position between the short run and long run.
- Fourth, find the **Equilibrium** price and quantity based on the profit-maximising position MC = MR. Draw a vertical line down from the MC = MR position to the Q axis to find the quantity. Draw a vertical line up from the MC = MR position as far as the AR curve. Then draw a horizontal line across to the P axis to find the price.
- Fifth and finally, if AR is greater than AC, **Supernormal profits** are being earned. Label the rectangle if necessary.

It is vital to treat the chapters on market structures as a 'family', as set out on the spectrum on page 54. Each one is best understood in relation to the others, so it is intended that you study them together, constantly comparing them as you do so.

key point

- Characteristics of oligopoly
- Equilibrium under oligopoly
- Definition of price rigidity and price constancy
- Methods of collusion
- Price leadership
- Reasons for non-profit maximisation
- How to draw market structure diagrams

exam Q

2016, Section B, Question 2 (a)
Cadbury, Mars and Nestlé dominate the chocolate industry in the European Union.
  (i) State a market structure which most closely reflects the situation above, giving a reason for your answer.
 (ii) Outline two other key characteristics of this market structure.
(iii) Explain, with the aid of a labelled diagram, the likely shape of the demand curve in this market structure.

Marking scheme
  (i)
- Market structure and reason @ 7 marks

 (ii)
- 2 characteristics @ 5 marks (2 + 3)

(iii)

- Diagram @ 5 marks
- Explanation @ 3 + 5 + 5 marks
- 35 marks in total

Answer

(i)

- Oligopoly is the market structure that most closely reflects this situation.
- This is due to the high concentration ratio, i.e. the market is dominated by a small number of large firms.

(ii)

- Barriers to entry exist. Firms in the industry do everything possible to keep new firms out, e.g. brand proliferation.
- The market is dominated by a small number of large firms.
- Firms engage in product differentiation by selling similar but unique products.
- There is a high degree of knowledge regarding profits and costs.
- Firms are interdependent. No firm alters its price without considering what its competitors will do in response.
- Collusion can occur, whereby firms agree to fix prices artificially high in order to increase every firm's profits.
- Firms aim to maximise profits, at MC = MR. However, firms may have objectives other than profit maximisation.

(iii)

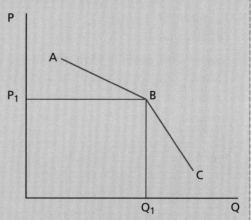

- The downward-sloping demand curve is kinked at point B, making it relatively elastic above the prevailing price and relatively inelastic below the prevailing price.
- For every 1% increase in price, quantity demanded will fall by more than 1%. This is because competing firms are assumed to leave their price unchanged, as a result taking customers from the firm that raised its price.
- For every 1% drop in price, quantity demanded will rise by less than 1%. This is because competing firms presumably will respond by lowering their price to match it.
- Either way, there is no incentive for the firm to alter its price from the prevailing price since both result in a fall in revenue.

2015, Section A, Question 4

A high concentration ratio is a key feature of an Oligopolistic Market.

(a) Explain this statement and give one example.

(b) Outline two ways oligopolists behave in the market.

Marking scheme

(a)

- Explanation @ 4 marks
- Example @ 2 marks

(b)

- 2 ways @ 4 marks each
- 16 marks in total

Answer

(a)

- A high concentration ratio means that a small number of large firms account for a high percentage of the total output of an industry.
- Example: The leading 5 grocery market chains in Ireland account for almost 90% of sales.

(b)

- **Non-price competition:** Reluctant to provoke rivals by lowering price, firms prefer non-price tactics such as loyalty card, extended opening hours etc.
- **Firms are interdependent:** Like in a game of rock-paper-scissors, firms always consider rival firms likely reactions to their own actions.
- **Collusion:** There is an incentive for firms to illegally act in concert for their mutual benefit, e.g. by setting a common price.

2013, Section A, Question 4

(a) Collusion may be a feature of an oligopolistic market. Explain what is meant by 'collusion'.

(b) Collusive practices may be undermined by price wars. Outline two benefits of price wars for the consumer.

Marking scheme

(a)

- Definition @ 8 marks

(b)

- 2 points @ 4 marks each

Answer

(a) Collusion occurs when firms secretly come together and cooperate for their mutual benefit.

(b)

- **Lower prices:** A price war leads to lower prices, greater value for money and a larger consumer surplus.
- **Higher disposable income:** The consumer has more money left over after their shopping, resulting in a higher standard of living.
- **Greater choice:** Given a greater disposable income, the consumer can now decide how to spend it.

13 Introduction to the Factors of Production

- To outline the importance of the factors of production
- To define supply price, transfer earnings, economic rent, and quasi-rent
- To distinguish between a specific and a non-specific factor of production
- To define derived demand
- To define MPP and MRP and their relationship
- To discuss the factors that shape the MRP curve

The factors of production

In order to supply any good or service, a firm requires **land**, **labour**, **capital** and **enterprise**.

- The markets for the factors of production function in much the same way as the markets for any other goods and services.
- We study them because they are four particularly important goods and services, since they're needed to make everything else.
- Price depends on the interaction of supply and demand.

Payments and returns

- The **supply price** of a factor is the minimum payment needed to bring it into use and keep it in that employment.
- The **transfer earnings** of a factor of production is the return it could earn in its next best employment.
- Any earnings in excess of the supply price are **economic rent**, which can be thought of as the **producer surplus** earned for the person supplying that factor. It is earnings in excess of the minimum the person is prepared to accept, e.g. if a business owner would be happy with €60,000 profit (her transfer earnings) but receives €80,000, her economic rent is €20,000.
- **Payment to a factor – transfer earnings = economic rent**.
- The ability to earn economic rent requires an element of monopoly power or an inelasticity of supply. No economic rent is earned in a perfectly competitive market.
- **Quasi-rent** is temporary economic rent, e.g. a sudden shortage of computer programmers during an economic boom. In the LR, it is eroded as more enter the market, but in the SR the supply of computer programmers is inelastic.
- The government sometimes will try to limit economic rent, either by taxing it or taking steps to increase the supply of that factor.

Specific and non-specific factors of production

- A **specific** factor of production is one with no alternative uses, e.g. a photocopier is only useful as a photocopier, nothing else.
- A **non-specific** factor of production can have multiple uses, e.g. a shop unit can be used for a pharmacy or for a health food shop.
- The more specific a factor of production, the greater the economic rent it earns. Since it has no alternative uses, it makes no transfer earnings. Everything it earns is economic rent.

Supply and demand

- The **supply** of the factors of production comes from people trying to earn a return:
  - The return on land is **rent**.
  - The return on labour is **wages**.
  - The return on capital is **interest**.
  - The return on enterprise is **profit**.
- The demand for the factors of production is a **derived demand**. No factor is demanded for its own sake, but only for the goods and services that it can be used to make, e.g. lumber is in demand only because it can be used to make paper, furniture, etc. The firm then hopes to sell those goods and services at a profit.

MPP and MRP

- The **Marginal Physical Product (MPP)** of a factor of production is the extra **output** produced as a result of employing one more unit of that factor, e.g. if output was 75 units before adding a worker, and 100 units afterwards, the MPP of that worker is 25 units.
  - MPP will depend on:
    - The Law of Diminishing Marginal Returns (see page 35)
    - The quality of the factor, e.g. a brilliant scriptwriter
    - The ability of the entrepreneur to combine the factors together
- The **Marginal Revenue Product (MRP)** of a factor of production is the extra **revenue** $(P \times Q)$ earned by the firm as a result of employing one more unit of that factor, e.g. if revenue was €150,000 before adding a worker, and €200,000 afterwards, the MRP of that worker is €50,000.
  - MRP will depend on:
    - MPP, since revenue depends directly on output
    - The selling price of the good or service
    - The elasticity of demand

> **exam focus**
>
> When defining either MPP or MRP, a common mistake is to say 'one more factor' (e.g. labour) rather than 'one more **unit** of a factor' (e.g. one more worker).

- **MPP $\times$ MR = MRP**, i.e. the extra output produced by a unit of a factor multiplied by the price (MR) that is received for that output equals the extra revenue generated by that unit.

- The maximum a firm will pay for one more unit of a factor is the revenue it can earn from that unit, e.g. if an extra salesperson can increase revenue by €80,000, then obviously a firm will pay the salesperson up to €80,000. Hence the MRP curve of a factor is the **demand curve** of that factor.
- One exception is **labour hoarding**, i.e. a firm will still employ a worker if it sees a fall in revenue as temporary, or if it thinks it will only have to rehire (and retrain) a worker later on.
- Like any normal demand curve, the MRP curve slopes **downward**:

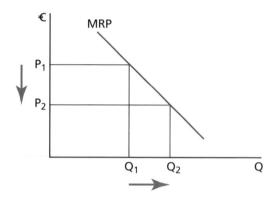

  - In monopoly and imperfect competition, the MRP curve slopes down for **two** reasons:
    - The Law of Diminishing Marginal Returns.
    - The Law of Demand. Since firms face a downward-sloping demand curve, they must lower the price (MR) in order to sell more units.
  - In perfect competition, it slopes downward for only **one** reason:
    - The Law of Diminishing Marginal Returns.
  - The Law of Demand does **not** apply. Since all firms are price takers, firms do not have to lower the price (MR) in order to sell more units.
  - The MRP curve of a firm in monopoly or imperfect competition will therefore slope downwards faster than the MRP curve of a firm in perfect competition.
  - Therefore, perfectly competitive firms usually demand more factors of production than monopolistic or imperfectly competitive firms.

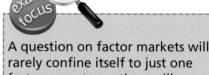

A question on factor markets will rarely confine itself to just one factor – most questions will examine two. As with the market structures, it's a good idea to study this 'family' of chapters together.

key point

- Importance of the factors of production
- Supply price, transfer earnings, economic rent and quasi-rent
- Derived demand
- MPP and the factors influencing it
- MRP and the factors influencing it
- The MRP curve and the factors affecting its slope under different market structures

2012, Section B, Question 3 (a)

(i) Explain the following terms in relation to a factor of production:
- Supply Price
- Transfer Earnings

(ii) Explain the concept Economic Rent and outline two circumstances under which a factor of production can earn it.

Marking scheme
- 2 definitions @ 5 marks each
- Definition of economic rent @ 5 marks
- 2 circumstances @ 5 marks each
- 25 marks in total

Answer
(i)
- **Supply Price:** The minimum payment necessary to bring a factor into use and keep it in that use.
- **Transfer Earnings:** The earnings a factor would make in its next best alternative employment.

(ii)
- **Economic Rent:** Any earnings a factor of production makes above its supply price/transfer earnings.
- Two circumstances under which it can be earned:
  - If a person has a rare **skill or talent** that is in high demand, e.g. a great scriptwriter.
  - If there is a **shortage** of a factor, e.g. development land, its owner can earn economic rent from it.
  - **Rent of Ability:** An entrepreneur who consistently provides the market with products that they desire.

The more **specific** a factor, by definition the fewer alternative uses it has, and therefore the lower its transfer earnings, e.g. a vacuum cleaner cannot be adapted to any other use.

2011, Section B, Question 3 (a)

(i) Define the term Marginal Revenue Productivity (MRP) of a factor of production.

(ii) State and explain two factors that can influence MRP.

(iii) Outline two difficulties that may arise in measuring MRP.

Marking scheme

- 5 marks for definition
- 2 factors @ 5 marks each
- 2 difficulties @ 5 marks each
- 25 marks in total

Answer

(i) The Marginal Revenue Product (MRP) is the additional revenue earned when one extra unit of a factor of production is employed.

(ii)

- **Selling price:** The higher the selling price of the product the factor contributes to, the higher will be the MRP of the factor.
- **Productivity of the factor:** The higher the level of output per additional unit of a factor, the higher will be its MRP, e.g. due to the commitment shown by a worker.
- **Quality of the factor:** Perhaps due to the unique talent of a worker or the greater efficiency of a machine, the higher the quality of the extra unit employed, the greater will be its MRP.
- **Entrepreneurial ability:** If the factors are organised into a production unit by an entrepreneur of exceptional ability, this will increase the MRP of each factor involved.
- **The Law of Demand:** To sell more, a producer usually must lower its price. This will directly impact on the MRP of the factors involved.
- **Training:** In the case of labour, the more training and education workers have received, the higher will be their MRP.
- **The Law of Diminishing Marginal Returns:** As more units of a variable factor are combined with a fixed factor, the addition to output – and to revenue in the form of MRP – of each additional unit of the variable factor can eventually decline.

(iii)

- MRP cannot always be measured. If services are provided, no physical output is produced.
- When production requires both labour and capital, it is difficult to distinguish between the role each factor plays.
- Much of the output of the public sector is not sold in the market. Therefore, it is difficult to calculate its MRP.

14 Land

- To define land
- To outline the characteristics of land
- To discuss the factors that influence the demand for land
- To explain the factors that influence a firm's location

Land

- It is anything we get from nature that is used in the production of goods and services.
- It includes agricultural land, water, minerals extracted from the ground, and even the weather.
- All production requires at least some land.
- The return earned by land is **rent**.

Characteristics of land

- **Fixed in supply**
  - Apart from the relatively small amounts of land reclaimed from the sea, the quantity of land is fixed. Its supply is perfectly inelastic.
  - Therefore, a change in its price (i.e. rent) is determined solely by demand.
  - Rent is in turn determined by the MRP of land, i.e. land will be rented to the bidder who can put it to its

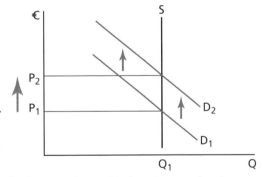

most profitable use, e.g. a luxury car dealer can charge high prices, and so is willing to pay high rent. The price determines the rent, not the other way about.

- **No cost of production**
  - Unlike the other factors, land is provided by nature and hence has no cost of production.
  - Therefore, all of the rent earned by land in general is **economic rent**, since the absence of a cost of production means there is no **transfer payment**, i.e. land can only be land.

- **Physically immobile**
  - Land is the only factor that cannot be moved from place to place. It is a non-portable commodity.

– Land is generally a **non-specific** factor of production, i.e. it has multiple uses. A butcher shop can be refitted as a café, a shopping centre can be built on what used to be farmland. Therefore, a specific piece of land can attract a transfer payment to switch it from one use to another.

Land can be divided into:

> **exam focus**
>
> Ensure that you are fully familiar with the characteristics unique to each factor of production. They regularly appear in questions on the factor markets.

- **Renewable land**: It is naturally replenished, e.g. forestry. However, if it is abused, a renewable resource can be lost.
- **Non-renewable land**: It can be used only once, e.g. oil.

Because of its importance, the government is heavily involved in regulating the use of land. It is **zoned** according to agricultural, residential, commercial or recreational use. This is done so that:

- Development takes place in an organised fashion, e.g. factories are grouped together rather than randomly dotted throughout residential areas
- Areas of natural beauty, e.g. Glendalough, are protected
- There are adequate green belts in urban areas, e.g. St. Stephen's Green

Demand for land

The demand for land is influenced by several factors:

- **Residential:** The demand for housing in turn influences land prices. Land is sometimes **rezoned** from agricultural to residential use in order to satisfy this demand.
- **Commercial:** Land is required to build shopping centres, offices and factories.
- **Agricultural:** Some of the demand for land comes from within the farming sector, as farmers wish to expand their holdings.
- **Government:** Land is needed for the construction of motorways, the building of schools and hospitals, government offices and semi-state bodies, and for setting aside for social housing.
- **Recreational:** There is a need for public parks, sports facilities, national parks, and for green areas in otherwise residential localities.
- **Speculation and property bubbles:** Demand for land and for houses in particular does not always obey the Law of Demand:
  - If prices are rising, people generally wish to purchase before house prices get even higher.
  - Such demand can also be fuelled by speculators who see a chance to buy now and sell at a profit later on.
  - This upward pressure on house prices can lead to a self-sustaining bubble, particularly if banks succumb to the temptation to relax their lending practices. As prices rise, people outbid each other to buy before prices rise higher – thereby sending them higher.
  - Such a bubble can be followed by a self-sustaining crash: As prices eventually stagnate and begin to fall, people then chose to wait until prices go lower – thereby sending them lower. Confidence among both lenders and borrowers plunges.
  - Ireland experienced an acute housing bubble in the first decade of this century, followed by a crash that led the government to take on the debts of the banks and borrow heavily to restore the national finances.

Location of firms

- **Supply-oriented (weight-losing) industries:** Access to raw materials is more important than proximity to the market, e.g. an oil company.
- **Market-oriented (weight-gaining) industries:** Being close to the market is more important than access to raw materials, e.g. a market gardener.
- **Footloose:** Firms are neither supply- nor market-oriented. They can locate anywhere, e.g. an internet-based company.

Location will also depend on:

- The availability of skilled labour at a competitive wage
- The availability of suitable transport
- Telecommunications (particularly broadband) and energy
- Government policy, e.g. availability of grants

Ireland's **advantages as a location** for multinational industry:

- English-speaking population
- Low corporation tax rate
- Educated workforce
- Membership of the EU Single Market and the Euro
- Stable political environment
- Pro-enterprise government policies
- Presence of other multinationals

key point

- Definition of land
- Characteristics of land
- Factors that influence the demand for land
- Reasons why firms locate where they do

2014, Section B, Question 4 (b)

(i) Outline two economic characteristics of 'land'.

(ii) Discuss three economic factors which influence a firm's decision on where to locate its operations within Ireland.

Marking scheme

- 2 characteristics @ 5 marks each
- 3 factors @ 5 marks each
- 25 marks in total

Answer

(i)

- **Land is fixed in supply**, meaning that the supply curve is vertical and therefore inelastic. The overall supply of land does not increase if a higher price is offered. While some land is reclaimed from the sea, it is a tiny percentage of all land.
- **Land has no cost of production to society as a whole**, since it is a gift of nature. Since this means that the supply price is zero, all rent earned is economic rent.
- **Land is a non-specific factor.** It can be switched from agricultural to residential to commercial use.

(ii)

- **Availability of skilled workers.** A firm will need to locate close to workers with whatever skills it needs, e.g. film production in Los Angeles.
- **Planning Laws.** Firms may be influenced by the size, height, permitted opening hours etc. of the factory they are allowed by law by build.
- **Proximity to other firms in the same industry.** Firms can gain from external economies of scale by locating close to other firms in the same industry, e.g. clusters of IT companies in Dublin.
- **Proximity to the market.** Businesses such as hotels or clothing retailers will wish to locate in city centre locations, close to their customers.
- **Proximity to raw materials.** On the other hand, weight-losing industries tend to locate close to their main raw materials, e.g. an oil refining company.
- **Adequate infrastructure.** Firms need access to good road, rail and air links, in addition to electricity, sewage and broadband services.
- **Government Grants and Incentives.** Firms can be influenced in their choice of location by government funding, advanced factories and other incentives. The Industrial Development Authority (IDA) attempts to use these factors to attract foreign multinationals to Ireland.
- **Social Infrastructure.** A location without adequate schools, hospitals and shops, in addition to an attractive lifestyle, will find it hard to attract workers. Firms may therefore be reluctant to choose it as a location.
- **Price of Commercial Property.** The price of property and levels of rent will influence the choice of location, e.g. a city centre or a suburban location.

15 Labour

<table>
aims
</table>

- To define labour
- To outline the factors that determine the supply and demand for labour
- To outline the factors affecting mobility of labour
- To explain why different workers earn different wage rates
- To discuss different types of unemployment

Labour

Labour is:

- Any human effort used in the production of goods and services

The return earned by labour is **wages**.

The **population** can be divided into two categories:

- Those available for work, called the **labour force**
- Those **not available for work**, such as children, retirees, those unable to work due to a long-term illness or disability, those in full-time education, and anyone who doesn't need or want to work

exam focus

Make sure to include the words 'in the production of goods and services', e.g. your Leaving Cert takes human effort, but goods or services are not being produced, so it isn't 'labour' in economic terms.

The **labour force** can be further split into two groups:

- Those in employment, i.e. the **work force**, including those who are on holiday or out sick
- The **unemployed**, i.e. those without jobs but who are actively seeking employment

Everyone in the work force is in the labour force (along with the unemployed); everyone in the labour force is in the population (along with those unavailable for work).

The **demand for labour** depends on:

- **Consumer demand**: The more demand a firm has for its products, the more workers it will hire (derived demand).
- **The MRP of labour**: Firms hire extra workers if the extra revenue they generate exceeds the extra wages.
- **MPP of labour**: The more an extra worker can add to output, the higher the demand for labour.

- **Capital**: There are two effects:
  - Labour's MPP rises when combined with capital, e.g. a farmer with a tractor has a much higher MPP than a farmer without a tractor.
  - Labour can also be replaced by capital, e.g. driverless cars.
- **Employer's PRSI**: Firms must pay PRSI for every employee, driving up the cost of hiring.
- **Government grants or subsidies**: Firms are sometimes incentivised by the government to hire workers.
- **Trade unions** could force an employer to stop hiring, in order to protect existing workers' wages.

The MRP curve (i.e. labour **demand curve**) slopes downward.

The **supply of labour** depends on:

- **The wage rate**: Higher wages attract more workers into the market, but also encourage *existing* workers to supply more labour, i.e. work more hours.
- **Population**: The greater the population, the greater the **labour force** and hence the greater the **work force**.
- **Working hours and holidays**: A longer working week and fewer holidays increase the supply of labour.
- **Participation rate**: The percentage of the population who choose to be in the labour force. It depends on:
  - The demand for labour and the wages on offer
  - Income tax rates, including marginal tax rates
  - The level of social welfare available
  - The statutory retirement age
  - The average school-leaving age
  - Numbers choosing to work in the home
  - Numbers in full-time third-level education

The **supply curve** for labour usually slopes upward. In a free market, the interaction of demand and supply will decide the wage rate:

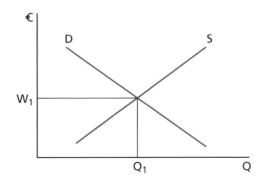

However, several other factors can influence the market:

- **Minimum wage legislation**: This makes it illegal to pay workers less than a certain wage. No labour can be supplied below that wage level. A related term, a **living wage**, is one which makes possible a minimum acceptable standard of living.

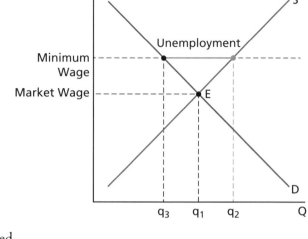

  A minimum wage increases unemployment. In the diagram, Q1 is the quantity traded in a free market. When the minimum wage is introduced, Q2 is supplied, but only Q3 is demanded, creating unemployment.

- **Backward-bending supply curve**: Beyond a certain wage, some workers will have enough earned and wish to spend time on leisure activities instead. Below the wage level W_1, the supply curve slopes upward as normal. As wages go above W_1, the supply of labour is reduced in favour of leisure time, e.g. a highly paid worker turning down an overtime opportunity in order to play golf instead.

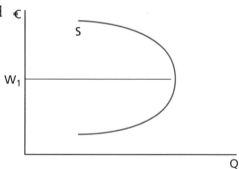

- **Trade union restriction on supply**: A union with monopoly power can restrict the number of workers in an industry, shift the supply curve left and drive up the wage rate. This is done by:
  - Limiting opportunities for graduates
  - Making training long and expensive
  - Setting difficult entry exams

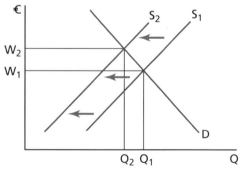

- **Wage drift**: An increase in labour demand drives wages up, but a fall in demand brings lay-offs rather than wage cuts because unions oppose them.

- **A wage freeze**, i.e. a government ban on wage increases, is sometimes imposed in order to control inflation. Firms instead compete for workers by other means, e.g. offering more overtime.

Mobility of labour has two varieties:

- **Occupational mobility** is the ease with which people can move from one job to another.
- **Geographic mobility** is the ease with which people can move from one place to another.

The greater the labour mobility, the lower the level of unemployment – both for the economy and for the individual. **SOLAS** is the government body that helps workers to improve their skills, increasing their labour mobility. Reasons for labour immobility include:

- Language or cultural barriers
- Trade union barriers such as a closed shop
- Lack of knowledge about available opportunities
- Lack of housing, or high rents
- The need for a high level of skill
- A reluctance to leave home or family, especially as the worker grows older
- Government policy on immigration, work permits, etc.

Wage rates

Different jobs pay different wages. This is due to:

- **Demand and supply**: If employers struggle to find workers with particular skills, they will have to offer a higher wage. If there is a large supply of suitable candidates, employers can offer a lower wage.
- **Productivity**: The higher the MPP (and hence the MRP) of a worker, the higher the wage they can earn.
- **Relativity and comparability**: Workers tend to look for pay rises when others with similar jobs have got them.
- **Experience and length of service**: The more experience a worker has, the less training and supervision is needed, and the higher the wage rate they can demand.
- **Working conditions**: If work is unpleasant or dangerous, or the hours are unsociable, the wage is often higher.
- **Rent of ability**: A person with an innate talent or ability can earn economic rent over and above other workers, e.g. a talented musician.
- **Monetary benefits**: Health insurance, pensions, cheaper loans if working for a bank, etc. The better these are, the lower the wage the employer needs to offer.
- **Benefits in kind**: The better the perks of a job, the lower the wage the employer needs to offer.
- **Trade union power**: An organised and united trade union can force an employer to pay higher wages.
- **Private vs. public sector**: Public sector wages tend to be more inflexible. In a boom, they are not the first to rise; in a recession they are not the first to fall. The public sector is more unionised, has historically greater job security, and has better pensions.

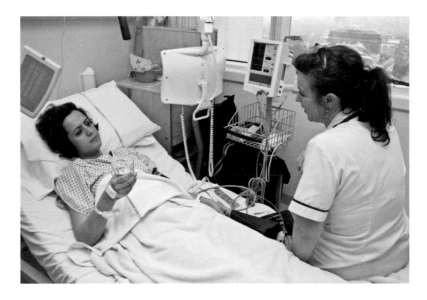

- **Permanency**: Usually permanent workers are paid more, although in some industries workers earn more by way of compensation for the uncertainty of temporary work.
- **Tradition**: If the MRP of a worker is hard to estimate, e.g. a nurse, established views as to the importance of their role can decide their pay. Measuring MRP is harder for firms providing a service than for ones selling a good, since there are no tangible products that can be counted or measured.
- **Length and cost of training**: Workers who require lengthy training demand higher wages as compensation. Training also makes them more valuable, increasing the wage the employer will be willing to pay, e.g. doctors.
- **Gender**: Despite much legislation, there are still pay differentials to be found between men and women.

The **MRP** of a worker depends on:

- Their **skills**, **abilities** and **experience**
- Their **dedication** and **commitment** to doing a good job
- Their **qualifications** and **training**
- Their ability to co-operate and **work with others**

It is also influenced by factors outside their control:

- The abilities of their **manager** and others around them
- Their **innate abilities**
- The **consumer demand** for what they are producing
- The **technology** and tools they use. It is not easy to distinguish between the MRP of labour and the MRP of capital
- The use of **specialisation** in the workplace

Specialisation: If you try to learn many skills, you can become good at a lot of them but expert at none. But if you focus on just one skill, and other workers focus on other skills, a better overall outcome can be achieved.

Advantages of specialisation

- Greater skill and speed
- Less time wasted switching between tasks
- Greater efficiency and output

Disadvantages of specialisation

- Boredom due to a lack of variety
- Restricted labour mobility
- Dependence on others with skills you don't have

Unemployment

- The **Live Register** includes everyone under 65 who gets Jobseeker's Benefit or Jobseeker's Allowance.
- Since it also includes part-time and casual workers and others, it is **not** a measure of unemployment, i.e. those without jobs who are actively seeking work.
- Unemployment is measured using the **Quarterly National Household Survey**.

Types of unemployment

- **Cyclical**: During recessions, firms sell less, and hence need fewer workers. All parts of the economy are affected at the same time.
- **Seasonal**: Some industries need fewer workers at certain times of the year, e.g. retailers hire extra staff at Christmas and lay them off again in January.
- **Frictional**:
  - People between jobs, usually for a short time
  - People seeking work but who don't have the skills for the jobs currently available
  - This occurs even when the economy is healthy
- **Institutional**:
  - Obstacles to the mobility of labour (see page 101)
  - A disincentive to work, e.g. low wages relative to social welfare
- **Structural**:
  - **New technology** replaces workers, e.g. the increasing use of robotics in industry
  - A **change in the pattern of demand** causes the decline of an industry, e.g. the effect of streaming and downloads on the music and movie industries

exam focus

Ensure going into your exam that you have up-to-date figures for employment and unemployment, along with the other main economic indicators. A question on the current state of the Irish economy will require you to quote relevant figures. Not all of the above types of unemployment may be relevant in the year you sit your Leaving Cert exam.

- **Underemployment**:
  - People who have work, but are not working at full capacity, e.g. people on a three-day week

Full employment occurs when everyone who is available for work at the present wage rate is employed. There is no cyclical unemployment, but there may be frictional unemployment.

- Definition of labour
- Factors that determine the supply and demand for labour
- Factors affecting mobility of labour
- Why different workers earn different wage rates
- Different types of unemployment

2016, Section A, Question 3
Outline two ways the Irish government could improve the mobility of labour in order to reduce unemployment.

Marking scheme
- 2 @ 8 marks each
- 16 marks in total

Answer
Occupational mobility

- **Retrain** workers with the educational qualifications and skills they need to move between professions.
- Remove professional and trade union **restrictions** which prevent workers from moving between jobs.
- Make it easier to obtain **permits** where required.

Geographical mobility

- Subsidise **relocation** expenses to enable workers to move around the country.
- **Inform** the public of the existence of vacancies they may be unaware of in other places.
- Build more affordable (social) **housing** and subsidise those who wish to buy or rent **accommodation**.
- Provide **social infrastructure** such as parks, schools, leisure facilities, etc. without which an area will not be an attractive prospect for relocation.

2016, Section B, Question 3 (a)

Explain the following terms in relation to the factor of production 'labour'.

(i) Participation rate

(ii) Real wages

(iii) Labour productivity

(iv) Derived demand

Marking scheme

- 8 marks for the 1st correct response
- 4 marks for the 2nd, 3rd and 4th responses
- Total: 20 marks

Answer

(i) **Participation rate**

The percentage of the working population between the ages of 16–65 who are either employed or seeking employment. Those in full-time education, choosing to work in the home or above the age of 65 are not considered to be in the labour force.

(ii) **Real wages**

The purchasing power of wages, i.e. the amount of goods and services the worker can buy with the nominal wage. If inflation rises but the wages don't change, real wages have nevertheless fallen.

(iii) **Labour productivity**

The output produced per worker over a period of time, e.g. in one year.

(iv) **Derived demand**

When factors of production are not demanded for their own sake but for their contribution to the production process.

2016, Section B, Question 3 (b) (i)

Discuss the factors that impact on the supply of labour.

Marking scheme

- Four points @ 5 marks each
- Total: 20 marks

Answer

- **The average working week/number of public holidays:** These vary between countries, and will directly influence the supply of labour in the economy in the year.
- **The backward bending supply of labour:** As wages rise beyond a certain level, some people may work less in order to pursue more leisure activities.
- **Wage levels abroad:** If wages are higher elsewhere, some workers will choose to emigrate rather than supply their labour in the Irish market.
- **The marginal rate of tax:** Employees may be reluctant to work overtime or pursue promotion if too much of the extra income earned is taxed.

- **Social welfare payments:** Unless wages sufficiently exceed the level of Jobseeker's Benefit, the unemployed may be reluctant to take up job opportunities. This may be seen as a reason to reduce Jobseeker's Benefit.
- **The minimum wage rate:** The higher the minimum wage, the more people will seek employment.
- **The participation rate:** Anything that increases the participation rate, such as social attitudes to women working outside the home, school-leaving age etc. will increase the supply of labour.
- **Labour mobility:** Greater geographic and occupational mobility of labour will increase the supply of labour in an economy.
- **Migration patterns:** The arrival of new people into Ireland, and the return of Irish people who previously emigrated, both increase the supply of labour.

aims
- To define capital and capital-related terms
- To explain the factors determining the level of investment
- To discuss the reasons why people save and the factors affecting the level of saving
- To outline the factors affecting the interest rate
- To explain the Classical Theory (Loanable Funds Theory) of interest rates
- To outline the Liquidity Preference Theory of interest rates

Capital

- It is anything made by man that is used in the production of goods and services.
- It includes machinery, buildings, stock, etc.
- Capital increases the MRP of labour.
- The return earned by capital is **interest**.

Other capital terms

- **Creating capital:** Giving up some current consumption – i.e. investment depends on saving.
- **Fixed capital**: Fixed assets, e.g. premises, vehicles, etc.

exam focus

Note that banks offer savers one rate of interest, and charge borrowers a higher rate. This 'spread' is one of the ways banks make money. When the rate of interest is mentioned in this book, for simplicity it refers to both rates as if they were equal.

- **Working capital**: Man-made raw materials and stocks, partly finished and finished goods.
- **Private capital**: Capital that is owned by either individuals or privately owned companies.
- **Social capital**: Capital owned by the public in general, e.g. roads, airports, etc.
- **Gross capital formation**: The total amount of capital created in the economy in one year.
- **Net capital**: Gross capital formation minus depreciation.
- **Depreciation**: Capital that is used up due to wear and tear to machinery, raw materials being used, etc.
- **The investment ratio**: Gross investment as a percentage of Gross Domestic Product (GDP).
- **Capital widening**: An increase in capital that leaves the ratio of capital to labour unchanged, i.e. capital and labour grow by the same proportion.
- **Capital deepening**: An increase in capital that increases the ratio of capital to labour, i.e. capital grows by a larger proportion than labour. Production becomes more capital intensive and less labour intensive.

Savings and investment

Banks act as a 'bridge' between those who save part of their income and those who wish to borrow for investment. When people save their money in a bank, this money is available to be borrowed by investors (see Chapter 22). So even though savers and investors are two different groups of people, investment is directly dependent on savings.

Why people save

- To purchase expensive goods, e.g. a racing bike
- To earn interest on their savings
- For unplanned expenses, e.g. a household appliance breaks down

- Because they lead a prudent lifestyle, i.e. once their needs and wants are satisfied, they may not feel the urge to spend the rest of their income
- To prepare for retirement, i.e. paying into a pension
- To accumulate a deposit for a house
- To be ready for investment opportunities that may suddenly arise, e.g. a sought-after premises comes up for sale

Factors affecting the level of saving

- **Rate of interest**: The higher the rate of interest, the greater the incentive to save.
- **Rate of inflation**: Inflation eats away at the **real interest rate**, e.g. a saver who earns 5% interest when the inflation rate is 2% really only earns 3%.
- **Consumer confidence**: The more fearful people are about the future of the economy – and the safety of their own jobs – the more they will save, regardless of the rate of interest available. Sadly, if enough people save for this reason, it reduces consumer demand and makes job losses more likely.
- **Income**: Many people in less developed countries save little or nothing, since they must spend everything they earn in order to survive. As income rises, less is needed for current consumption. However, it can still be swallowed up by spending on luxuries.
- **Social welfare and pensions**: When support is available from the State to the unemployed and the retired, the need for personal saving is reduced.
- **Deposit Interest Retention Tax (DIRT)**: The higher the tax on interest, the less people will wish to save.

Factors affecting the level of investment

- **Rate of interest**: All else being equal, a rise in interest rates will result in less investment.
- **Expectations**: Investment depends on the level of optimism about future consumer demand, i.e. the expected rate of return on the investment. This is a more important factor than the rate of interest.
- **Government policy**: The government can encourage investment through grants, subsidies and a low rate of corporation tax.
- **Good infrastructure**: This is a requirement of international investors, e.g. motorways, adequate ports and airports, broadband, etc.
- **Ireland's membership of the EU and the Euro**: Ireland has become an attractive location for multinational companies, e.g. from the US. As the UK exits the EU, some firms are likely to relocate to Ireland.
- **Capital costs**: The higher the cost of capital goods (e.g. machinery), the more reluctant business people are to invest. Improvements in technology increase the productivity of capital and therefore encourage investment.
- **The Marginal Efficiency of Capital (MEC)**: The extra profit earned as a result of employing one more unit of capital.
- **Labour availability and wage levels**: Investment depends on a supply of highly skilled and educated workers. Ireland's status as an English-speaking country also attracts foreign companies. However, high wage rates can discourage investment.

- **The international economic situation**: Investment in a small open economy like Ireland is influenced greatly by international conditions outside our control.

Factors affecting the rate of interest

- **The Monetary Policy of the European Central Bank (ECB)**: The ECB decides the base rate for the Eurozone area, which heavily influences the rate banks charge borrowers (see Chapter 22).
- **Rate of inflation**: If inflation is high, the ECB will increase the interest rate in order to combat it (see Chapter 18). In addition, banks will wish to charge a higher rate than the rate of inflation in order to earn a real interest rate.
- **Demand for loans**: The greater the demand for loans, the higher the rate of interest, since borrowers compete with each other for available funds.
- **Credit rating of the borrower**: The riskier the track record of the borrower and the riskier the purpose of the loan, the higher the rate of interest.
- **Time span of loan**: The longer the loan is for, the higher the rate of interest, since the lender has to part with their money for longer. Also, a saver who wants the option of withdrawing their money on demand will earn a lower interest rate than someone prepared to give a longer period of notice.

Whenever you see lists like these, you should think in terms of potential exam questions and marking schemes. Implement the exam technique outlined in the Introduction.

- **Security**: A borrower who offers the deeds to a house as collateral will pay a lower rate of interest than someone who takes out an unsecured loan.

How interest rates are determined

The classical theory (loanable funds theory)

- The **supply curve** of loanable funds slopes upward. The higher the interest rate, the higher the level of saving.
- The **demand curve** slopes downward. Less is borrowed as the cost of borrowing increases.
- The **interest rate** is determined by the intersection of the demand and supply curves, just as in Chapter 4.
- The loanable funds theory has many drawbacks:
  - Borrowers are more influenced by expectations and the rate of the return on investment than they are by the rate of interest.

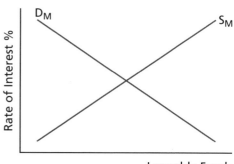

- As we have already seen, the rate of interest is not the only reason people save.
- The **primary liquidity ratio** will also influence how much banks can lend (see Chapter 22).

Theory of liquidity preference (John Maynard Keynes)

The **supply curve of money** is vertical and inelastic. This is because the overall money supply is decided by the ECB and is not determined by the interest rate.

The **demand curve for money,** according to Keynes, is actually made up of three demand curves. These three demand curves depend on three motives (or reasons) for wanting to hold money in **liquid form**, i.e. either in cash or in a form easily convertible into cash, e.g. a deposit account.

These three motives are:

- **The transactions motive**: Regardless of the rate of interest on offer in the bank, people will always hold some money in liquid form for day-to-day spending ('walking-around money'). Hence the **transactionary demand curve** is perfectly inelastic (i.e. unresponsive to interest rate changes).
- **The precautionary motive**: People need money in liquid form for emergencies (the 'rainy day'), but optimists may be tempted by a rise in interest rates to place some of it in illiquid form. The result is a downward-sloping **precautionary demand curve**.
- **The speculative motive**: People will keep a certain amount of money in liquid form in order to take advantage of investment opportunities that might arise, i.e. an investment opportunity that pays a better return than the rate of interest. As the rate of interest rises, less money is held for this purpose since the chances of earning a better return than the interest rate diminish. Hence, the **speculative demand curve** also slopes downward.

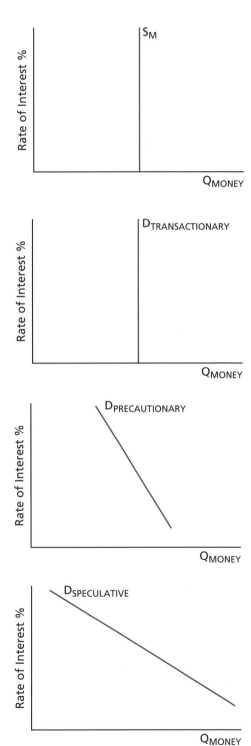

The sum (or aggregate) of the three demand curves (transactionary, precautionary and speculative) gives us a downward-sloping curve for **aggregate (overall) demand for money**. The rate of interest will be decided by where this downward-sloping demand curve intersects with the inelastic supply curve.

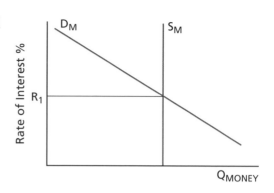

key point

- Definition of capital and capital-related terms
- Reasons why people save
- Factors affecting the level of saving
- Factors determining the level of investment
- Factors affecting the interest rate
- Classical Theory (Loanable Funds Theory) of interest rates
- Liquidity Preference Theory of interest rates

exam Q

2015, Section B, Question 4 (b)
(i) Distinguish between the terms capital and investment as used by economists.

Marking scheme
- 2 explanations @ 5 marks each
- 10 marks in total

Answer
- **Capital** is anything made by man that is used in the production of goods and services, i.e. the stock of machinery and equipment that a firm currently owns.
- **Investment** is the addition of new capital goods to the stock of capital a firm owns. This is also called capital formation, e.g. purchasing new machinery or constructing a new factory.

2015, Section B, Question 4 (c)
(i) State and explain the three motives put forward by John Maynard Keynes for holding assets in the form of cash.
(ii) Outline one main influence on each motive.

Marking scheme
- 3 motives @ 5 marks each
- 15 marks in total

Answer
- **Transactionary:** People need a certain amount of money for day-to-day purchases. It is unaffected by the rate of interest. The greater a person's income, the greater the transactions motive.
- **Precautionary:** People keep some money in liquid form in case of unforeseen circumstances, e.g. sudden illness, car repairs, etc. It will be somewhat influenced by the rate of interest.
- **Speculative:** People keep some funds in liquid form to take advantage of investment opportunities which may arise. The higher the rate of interest, the less likely it is that such opportunities will yield a better return than the rate of interest, so the less money that is kept for this purpose.

2013, Section A, Question 2
Define the 'Marginal Efficiency of Capital' (MEC). Outline **two** possible reasons for a fall in MEC.

Marking scheme
- Definition @ 8 marks
- Any 2 reasons @ 4 marks each
- 16 marks in total

Answer
The Marginal Efficiency of Capital (MEC) is the additional profit earned by employing one extra unit of capital.
Possible reasons why the MEC may fall:
- A rise in the cost of capital
- A fall in the price of the finished goods
- A rise in interest rates
- A decline in the productivity of capital
- A deterioration in the capital goods used

17 Enterprise

aims
- To define the entrepreneur
- To outline the characteristics of enterprise
- To discuss the role of enterprise in the economy
- To outline the role of profit in the economy

The entrepreneur

The entrepreneur (the person providing the enterprise):

- Organises the other three factors (land, labour and capital) into a business unit
- Attempts to anticipate consumer demand and come up with products and services to satisfy that demand
- Takes the risks in starting and running a business
- Can be a sole trader, partnership, co-operative, private limited company, public limited company, joint venture or even a government
- Pays an **implied cost** of enterprise in order to set up in business – the income the owner would be earning if they'd stayed in their old job, e.g. quitting a job in an insurance company to set up a crèche
- Earns a return or **profit**

Risks of entrepreneurship

The risks that entrepreneurs take can be divided into:

- **Insurable risks:**
  - Damage due to fire or weather
  - Public liability
  - Employer's liability
  - Product liability
  - Theft, by either customers or staff
  - Bad debts
- **Non-insurable risks:**
  - Industrial disputes
  - Loss of profits due to higher costs
  - Entry of rival firms into the industry
  - Stock produced that fails to sell

- Changes in consumer tastes
- Recession
- Unfavourable laws or regulations

Characteristics of enterprise

- Profit is **residual**. Rent, wages and interest are paid first. Anything left over is profit. If nothing is left over, the entrepreneur gets nothing.
- Even worse, enterprise is the only factor that can earn a **negative return**. The lowest that rent, wages or interest can go is 0. A profit can become a loss.
- Profit **fluctuates**. Rent, wages and interest remain relatively stable over time. Profits rise and fall in response to market conditions.

exam focus

Just as wages vary for different types of workers, entrepreneurs will earn varying levels of profit.

Enterprise under different economic systems

- **Free market economy**: Enterprise is provided by private individuals motivated by profit. They are also liable for any losses they incur.
- **Centrally planned economy**: The government is the entrepreneur on behalf of the people. Without an individual **profit motive**, there may be less innovation, more waste and a larger bureaucracy.
- **Mixed economy**: Private enterprise produces most things, but the State intervenes to ensure vital services are provided even if they make a loss.

The importance of the entrepreneur to an economy

- Provides us with a variety of goods and services
- Organises the other three factors
- Creates jobs and generates economic growth
- Contributes revenue to the government
- Sponsors community and cultural activities, e.g. sports teams

- Exports goods, improving Ireland's balance of trade
- Inspires others to become entrepreneurs
- Reduces reliance on the government to solve problems
- Reduces reliance on foreign multinationals here

Factors favouring the growth of enterprise

- Low corporation tax rates
- A pro-business regulatory and legal environment
- Low interest rates
- A stable economic and political environment
- High disposable income among consumers
- A culture of business ownership, optimism and imagination

The role of profit in the economy

- Encourages **risk-taking** and encourages firms to research and satisfy **customer needs and wants**.
- Signals how effectively this is being done. Going into business is the best form of market research.
- Encourages **efficiency** and **innovation**.
- Provides funds for **expansion**. Retained earnings are the cheapest source of capital – provided shareholders are agreeable.
- **Corporation tax** on profits funds government spending.
- Profit also tells **investors** where to allocate their wealth for maximum return. In the LR, investment flows to entrepreneurs with a proven track record. The higher return these entrepreneurs earn is called **rent of ability**.
- **Normal profit** must be earned in the LR to justify staying in business.

> Lowering Ireland's corporation tax from 40% to 12.5% during the 1990s played a major role in the 'Celtic Tiger'. It resulted in a huge growth in multinational companies locating here, and a growth in business ownership in general. This growth more than compensated for the lower rate of tax, so the government experienced a large rise in revenue.

- Definition of enterprise
- Risks facing entrepreneurs
- Characteristics of enterprise
- Enterprise under different economic systems
- Importance of enterprise to the economy
- Factors favouring the growth of enterprise
- Role of profit in the economy

2015, Section B, Question 4 (a)

(i) State and explain two economic characteristics of enterprise as a factor of production.

(ii) Explain the importance of profits in a market economy.

Marking scheme

- 2 characteristics @ 5 marks each (2 + 3)
- 4 points @ 5 marks each (2 + 3)
- 30 marks in total

Answer

(i) Characteristics of enterprise:

- Profit is residual. The entrepreneur only gets to keep what is left over after all the other factors have been paid their return.
- The entrepreneur is the only factor of production that can earn a loss.
- Profit fluctuates much more than the return to the other factors, which are often fixed as part of a contract.

(ii) The importance of profit in a market economy.

- **Provides revenue for the government:** Corporation tax collected on company profits helps to fund government services and improvements in infrastructure.
- **Incentivises entrepreneurship:** Profits are the reason entrepreneurs set up and expand businesses. Without profit, there would be no point in taking a risk.
- **Provides funds for expansion:** Retained earnings can be ploughed back into a successful business, enabling it to grow over time.
- **Indicates the best use of resources:** Profits or the lack of them signal to entrepreneurs how well they are responding to the demands of consumers.
- **Encourages investment:** The availability of profits encourages more firms to enter the market, creating jobs and wealth in the process.
- **Rewards innovation:** Entrepreneurs who generate new ideas, lower costs and deliver great service earn higher supernormal profits.

2014, Section A, Question 7

Outline two ways in which the return to the factor of production enterprise differs from the return to other factors of production.

Marking scheme

- 10 marks for 1st correct response
- 7 marks for 2nd correct response
- 17 marks in total

Answer

- **It can earn a negative return:** Unlike the other three factors, which at worst can earn a zero return, the entrepreneur risks losing money.
- **Returns can fluctuate:** Even when a firm is successful, profits can still vary widely from year to year.
- **Profit is residual:** Even though the entrepreneur is the one who generates the idea and starts the business, they must pay the other factors first. If there is nothing left over, the entrepreneur gets nothing.

PART TWO

Macroeconomics

18 The Role of Government in the Economy

- To describe the various economic policies the government can use to achieve its aims
- To set out the economic aims of government, and the policies that can be used for each aim
- To highlight how these different aims can come into conflict with one another
- To discuss the advantages and disadvantages of privatisation

Note that while this chapter explains many economic policies and problems, the questions you will be asked and the answers you will be required to give will depend on the economic conditions in the year you sit your exam. Therefore, you cannot simply learn this chapter by heart and reproduce it on the day. It is like a tool kit – you bring it with you everywhere, but the tools you use are determined by the problems you need to solve.

Economic policies

In order to achieve its objectives the government has the following tools or policies at its disposal:

- **Fiscal policy**: This means adjusting either government revenue (i.e. taxes) or spending or both. It is the most powerful tool our government has. It can be used to:
  - Encourage investment in certain industries or regions
  - Redistribute wealth through taxation and social welfare
  - Fund vital services, e.g. education, health, etc.
  - Invest in infrastructural projects
- **Legislation**: The government can pass new laws to:
  - Set a minimum wage
  - Control prices
  - Restrict monopolies or oligopolies
  - Protect the right of consumers
  - Regulate how industries work, e.g. banks
- **Market intervention**: The government becomes a competitor or even the sole operator in an industry, e.g. trains. Many socially desirable but unprofitable services would not be provided unless the government did so.
- **Social partnership**: This involves brokering pay agreements between employers and union representatives on a national basis with the aim of reducing industrial conflict and uncertainty regarding future pay increases.
- **Exchange rate policy** involves trying to influence the value of the currency relative to other currencies and is outside our government's control.
  - It can be adjusted via a **devaluation** (making the currency worth less in terms of other currencies) or a **revaluation** (making it worth more in terms of other currencies). A devaluation makes our exports cheaper; a revaluation makes our imports cheaper.
  - Because Ireland is a member of the Euro, this is controlled by the **European Central Bank (ECB)**.
- **Monetary policy**: This means controlling the money supply by means of the interest rate, with the objective of achieving price stability and stable economic growth, which is also outside our government's control.
  - Because Ireland is in the Euro, this is also controlled by the ECB. It has, however, a major impact on Ireland.

When the ECB raises interest rates

Who is affected:	Direct effect	Indirect effect
Consumers	Loans and credit cards cost more	Wish to borrow & spend less, but save more
Savers	The interest they earn goes up	Wish to save more & hence spend less
Borrowers	Loan repayments increase	Wish to borrow less, & hence spend less
Mortgage holders	Their mortgage repayments increase	Forced to reduce spending in other areas
Businesses	Loans cost more	Less willing to borrow in order to invest

As a result of these combined effects, demand for goods and services is reduced, and inflation in turn is reduced.

When the ECB lowers interest rates

Who is affected:	Direct effect	Indirect effect
Consumers	Loans and credit cards cost less	Willing to spend more
Savers	The interest they earn goes down	Less willing to save, more willing to spend
Borrowers	Loan repayments decrease	More willing to borrow & spend more
Mortgage holders	Their mortgage repayments decrease	More money to spend on other things
Businesses	Loans cost less	More willing to borrow in order to invest

As a result of these combined effects, demand for goods and services is increased, hopefully leading to economic growth. Of course, if it is overdone, you get inflation and have to raise the interest rate again. The ECB has to try to find a balance between low inflation and economic growth.

The economic aims of government

Now that we know what policies are available, we can look at the various aims of government, and how these policies can be used to achieve them:

- **Economic growth** is an increase in output per person in the economy. When output per person rises, income per person rises. More goods and services can be consumed, and the standard of living increases. However, economic growth does not come without costs (Chapter 27).

- **Policies**:
  - ▸ Reduce the interest rate to make it easier to borrow and hence invest.
  - ▸ Increase government spending to stimulate the economy.
  - ▸ Reduce corporation taxes to encourage companies to expand.
  - ▸ Reduce direct and indirect taxes to encourage consumer spending.
- **Managing the public finances**. If government spending exceeds revenue, the result is a budget deficit.
  - **Policies**:
    - ▸ Cut government spending.
    - ▸ Increase tax revenue, with the risk that higher tax rates may disincentivise work and investment. Depending on the **elasticity**, *lowering* tax rates may actually lead to *higher* tax revenue.
    - ▸ Borrow. The higher the National Debt, the higher the cost in interest payments to future taxpayers. Borrowing cannot continue indefinitely.

The government usually opts for some combination of all three. In the long run, however, it must balance the budget.

- **Adequate infrastructure**. A country needs roads, rail, broadband, water, sewage systems, harbours, airports, etc. The government often has to provide these because:
  - Many projects, though vital, don't return a profit, so private firms are not interested.
  - Infrastructure such as the LUAS costs more than most private firms can afford to finance. Some projects are jointly financed through **Public-Private Partnerships**.
  - Projects such as the motorways require co-ordination at a national level, multiple land purchases, etc.
  - **Policies**:
    - ▸ Direct government spending on infrastructure.
    - ▸ Public-private partnerships, e.g. share the cost of building a new motorway with a private firm, allowing that firm to collect the tolls for a set period of time.
- **Low inflation (price stability)**. Inflation erodes the competitiveness of our exports and reduces the spending power of consumers, especially those of fixed incomes.

- **Policies**:
    - ‣ Negotiate national pay agreements with the social partners that include modest pay increases.
    - ‣ Impose a wage freeze.
    - ‣ Impose price controls.
    - ‣ Increase interest rates, making saving more attractive and borrowing less attractive. As already stated, only the ECB can do this.
    - ‣ Increase direct taxes to cut consumer spending.
    - ‣ Reduce VAT, thereby cutting prices and hence inflation.
    - ‣ Reduce government spending.
- **Full employment** occurs when everyone who is available for work at the present wage rate is employed. It is not the same as zero unemployment, since there will always be people temporarily unemployed while between jobs.
    - **Policies**:
        - ‣ Increase public sector employment, e.g. nurses, Gardaí.
        - ‣ Train and upskill the unemployed.
        - ‣ Use grants and a low corporation tax rate to attract multinational companies here.
        - ‣ Reduce income taxes to encourage workers to take up jobs. Increased disposable income creates spin-off jobs.
        - ‣ Reduce indirect taxes, again to encourage spending.
        - ‣ Encourage firms to create jobs by reducing employer's PRSI.
        - ‣ Lower interest rates, increasing the availability of loans for business expansion.
        - ‣ Devalue the Euro to increase exports (only the ECB can do this)
        - ‣ Encourage wage restraint through social partnership agreements.
- **Equilibrium on the balance of payments** occurs when imports and exports are roughly equal. If the Eurozone imports more than it exports, the Euro will fall in value because we are spending more on imports than the rest of the world is spending on our exports. This increases the supply of the Euro, causing its price to drop. If exports exceed imports, the Euro rises in value, and the money that pours in causes inflation. Governments prefer a situation where imports and exports are roughly equal.
    - **Policies**:
        - ‣ Devalue the currency to make exports cheaper abroad and imports more expensive at home (only the ECB can do this).
        - ‣ Increase taxes on imports.
        - ‣ Give subsidies to exporting firms.
- **Social fairness**. Governments are committed to providing basic services to all citizens, regardless of economic status, e.g. 'free' education. These are called **merit goods**. Also, since a free market seems to naturally involve inequality of income, the government tries to redistribute some wealth from the rich who can afford it to the poor who depend on it.

- **Policies**:
  - ▸ Increase income tax rates for high earners.
  - ▸ Cut VAT on essential items, increase VAT on luxury goods.
  - ▸ Provide adequate social welfare payments.
  - ▸ Make funds available for the disabled.
  - ▸ Provide education grants for the less well-off.
- **Regional development**. Economic development tends to be concentrated around major urban areas where the largest markets are located, e.g. the greater Dublin area. The government tries to redirect some of this activity to other parts of the country that are neglected. This also eases congestion in Dublin.
  - **Policies**:
    - ▸ Provide grants for firms to locate in the BMW (Border, Midlands, and the West) region.
    - ▸ Invest in broadband, motorways and regional airports.
    - ▸ Decentralise government departments outside Dublin.
    - ▸ Encourage tourists – both Irish and foreign visitors – to travel outside of Dublin.

Conflicts between economic policies

There are many examples of how a policy designed to achieve one objective can adversely affect the achievement of another objective, i.e. there are opportunity costs:

- Increased government spending and lower interest rates are good for employment but also lead to inflation. Attempting to cut inflation can also cost jobs.
- Increased government spending creates employment but if the increase in income creates a demand for imports, it worsens the balance of payments.
- Social fairness requires higher taxes on the rich, but this can discourage investment and hence cost jobs. This dampens economic growth.
- On the other hand, policies that encourage economic growth, while beneficial to most, also increase inequality and the demand for income redistribution.
- If social welfare payments are higher than take-home pay, people are discouraged from taking up jobs. This is called the poverty/unemployment trap.
- Borrowing can make sense if it creates jobs, stimulates demand and finances infrastructure, but it also adds to the National Debt and contributes to inflation.

Economic policies can be compared with the levers and buttons on a complicated, slow and unpredictable machine:

- You do not have the resources to do everything you want. There are opportunity costs, so you must choose your priorities, e.g. build a hospital or cut taxes?
- The government can greatly influence the economy but it does not fully control it. People often have unrealistic expectations about what a government can do, e.g. the Irish government has no influence on oil prices.
- As a small open economy, much of what happens here is decided by the outside world, e.g. demand in the UK, US and elsewhere for our exports.

- Every action will have unforeseen consequences, both good and bad, e.g. economic growth causes traffic congestion and damages the environment.
- New challenges and problems are always arising, e.g. housing shortages, climate change.
- Governments are run by politicians, whose short-term goal is re-election. In theory, policy should be aimed at benefiting the common good, but governments are also tempted by a desire to please the electorate, e.g. by increasing spending coming up to an election.

Privatisation

Privatisation involves selling a state-owned company to the private sector, e.g. Telecom Eireann was privatised in 1999.

Advantages of privatisation

- Private owners, motivated by profit, may run the company more efficiently.
- The state no longer has to support a loss-making enterprise.
- Proceeds of the sale of state companies can be used to fund other government policies.
- The public may be able to purchase shares in the new privately owned company.

Disadvantages of privatisation

- The private sector is only interested in profitable opportunities. Socially desirable but unprofitable services, e.g. rural internet access, may be neglected.
- The private company may end up in foreign ownership.
- Jobs may be lost as the newly private company aims to reduce costs.
- A privatised monopoly is still a monopoly.

Nationalisation

Nationalisation is the opposite of privatisation, i.e. it involves the government transferring a previously privately owned firm into public ownership. Much of Ireland's banking industry was nationalised following the 2008 financial crisis. The government began the process of re-privatising the banks in 2017.

This chapter should be studied in tandem with Chapter 25, since the history of economics includes the history of economic policy.

- Economic policy options available to governments
- Economic aims of government
- How economic aims can come into conflict
- Advantages and disadvantages of privatisation

2016, Section A, Question 7

The primary aim of the ECBs monetary policy is to maintain price stability.

(a) Define the term monetary policy.

(b) Outline two benefits of price stability for the Irish economy.

Marking scheme

- Definition @ 9 marks
- 2 benefits @ 4 marks each
- 17 marks in total

Answer

(a) Monetary policy comprises the actions of the ECB which influence the money supply, interest rates and the availability of credit in the Eurozone economy.

(b)

- **Wage stability:** When prices are stable, workers don't seek wage increases. This encourages investment due to greater certainty about costs.
- **Value of money:** The purchasing power of money isn't eroded, which leads to a higher standard of living.
- **Competitiveness:** If Eurozone inflation is lower than inflation elsewhere, our exports become more competitive.
- **Consumer demand:** Low inflation means that consumers' money goes further, increasing consumer demand and thus creating jobs and economic growth.
- **Government revenue:** Increased demand generates more tax revenue, leading to better public services.
- **Savings:** The real rate of interest may be higher, so people may save more.

2016, Section B, Question 7 (b)

(i) Outline two economic policies which the Irish Government could consider to address inequality in Ireland.

(ii) Policies introduced to reduce inequality may make it more difficult for the government to achieve other economic aims. Explain this statement, using examples to support your answer.

Marking scheme

- 2 policies @ 8 marks each (3 + 5)
- 2 difficulties @ 7 marks each (3 + 4)
- 30 marks in total

Answer:

(i)

- **Merit goods:** We could ensure that certain services, such as education and health are available to all regardless of means, and ensure that electricity, water and other vital services are provided to all.
- **Create more jobs:** The government could increase employment by directly hiring more workers, e.g. Gardaí, by investing in infrastructure, cutting employers PRSI and other measures.
- **Social welfare:** Those on lower incomes could be given great social welfare payments, e.g. taking means into account when allocating child benefit payments.
- **Minimum Wage:** This would increase the standard of living for those on low pay, but it could impede job creation by making it more expensive to hire workers.
- **Taxation:** A progressive tax policy would take a higher percentage of income as incomes increase. A wealth tax could be considered, so that those who can afford to pay more would. Tax reliefs and shelters for higher earners could be abolished.
- **Training:** Up-skilling opportunities could be provided to the long-term unemployed, making them more employable. Those willing to take up jobs could still receive social welfare payments for a transitionary period.

(ii)

- **May cause budget deficit:** Spending more money to reduce unemployment may negatively affect the state finances.
- **Impact on economic growth:** Increased taxation to redistribute wealth may disincentivise entrepreneurship and investment. High earners may relocate elsewhere.
- **Disincentive to take up jobs:** Increased social welfare payments may discourage some who are unemployed from returning to the workforce.
- **Disincentive to remain working:** Higher marginal tax rates may 'punish' those on higher incomes, discouraging some from working overtime, pursuing promotion, or staying in employment altogether.
- **Inflation:** If more jobs are created, this results in higher spending, possibly leading to higher inflation.
- **Balance of Payments:** Job growth can also result in greater spending on imports, resulting in a deficit in our balance of payments.

2015, Section B, Question 8 (b)

(i) Outline three policies the Irish government could consider to achieve balanced regional development.

(ii) Outline two economic benefits to rural communities of balanced regional development.

Marking scheme

- 3 policies @ 5 marks each
- 2 benefits @ 5 marks each
- 25 marks in total

Answer

(i)

- **Infrastructure investment:** The government could continue the development of the motorway and train networks, invest in regional airports, and upgrade the electricity supply in less developed regions.
- **Broadband:** High speed internet access is a requirement for large firms to locate outside of major urban centres. It also makes it possible for many people to work from home, e.g. an interpreter could work with clients in the United States and continental Europe but live in County Sligo.
- **Grants & tax incentives:** Grants or tax breaks could encourage firms to locate in underdeveloped regions.
- **Training and education:** Firms are more likely to locate outside of our cities if the government invests in third-level institutions in regional areas.
- **Help for business start-ups:** Enterprise Ireland and other agencies could assist businesses that wish to set up in rural Ireland, e.g. start-up capital.

(ii)

- **Services:** Essential local services such as schools, post offices and hospitals are maintained.
- **Jobs:** Employment is created and retained in rural areas. As a result, more money is spent locally, leading to further job creation.
- **Reduced emigration and urbanisation:** People feel less compelled to move to cities or to leave Ireland entirely for work. The urban-rural divide is reduced.
- **Strong communities:** Rural areas become more attractive places to live, boosting not just economic but also sporting and cultural life.

19 Taxation and Government Debt

- To set out the reasons for taxation
- To outline Adam Smith's Canons of Taxation and the characteristics of a good tax system
- To define progressive and regressive tax
- To define direct and indirect taxation and describe some of their characteristics
- To distinguish between tax avoidance and tax evasion
- To distinguish between the incidence of a tax and the imposition of a tax
- To discuss the National Debt

Reasons for taxation

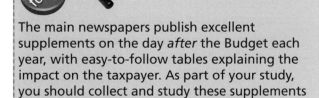

- **Fund government spending**: The government cannot provide education, health services, etc. without taxation.
- **Redistribute wealth**: Taxation is used to take income from those who can afford it in order to provide social welfare to those who cannot get by without it.

exam focus

The main newspapers publish excellent supplements on the day *after* the Budget each year, with easy-to-follow tables explaining the impact on the taxpayer. As part of your study, you should collect and study these supplements and the useful figures they contain.

- **Built-in stabiliser**: When the economy grows, tax revenues also grow, which has the effect of curbing inflation.

An Roinn Airgeadais
Department of Finance

- **Incentivise desirable behaviour**: Tax breaks or tax cuts can be used to encourage investment and employment, in turn encouraging economic growth.
- **Disincentivise socially undesirable behaviour**: The tax system can be used to 'punish' those who smoke, drive cars with large engine capacities, etc.

The canons of taxation (Adam Smith)

- **Equity**: The higher your income, the higher the proportion that should be paid in tax. Ability to pay should matter.
- **Certainty**: People should know in advance what the tax rates will be, allowing them to plan their spending and investment.
- **Convenience**: The method and timing of payment should be convenient to the taxpayer, not the government.
- **Economy**: The cost to the government of collecting a tax should be a small fraction of what is collected.

In addition, a good tax system should also have the following features:

- Taxes should not disincentivise work or investment. If marginal tax rates are too high, workers may not wish to work overtime or pursue promotion, and entrepreneurs may be reluctant to start or expand businesses.
- The tax system should be used to redistribute income from those who can afford it to those who need social welfare in order to survive. This should not disincentivise either the taxpayer or the welfare recipient from working.
- Tax evasion should be as hard to get away with as is practically possible.

Direct and indirect taxation

Direct taxation is a tax on income. It is paid directly to the government by those on whom it is imposed, e.g. PAYE, PRSI, USC, corporation tax, capital gains tax, capital acquisitions tax.

- It is progressive, i.e. the higher your income, the higher the rate you pay. Ability to pay is taken into account.
- High **marginal tax rates** can disincentivise work, e.g. if you are offered overtime or a promotion, but must pay half of your extra earnings in tax, you may not bother taking it up.

- Ireland's low corporation tax rate has encouraged investment, particularly from foreign multinationals.
- The cost of collecting PAYE and PRSI is borne by the employer, so it is cheap for the government to collect and normally convenient for the taxpayer to pay.
- High tax rates may encourage tax evasion and the black economy.
- The rates are announced in the Budget each year, and thus follow the principle of certainty.
- Direct tax rates act as an in-built stabiliser. More tax is collected in a growth period, less is collected in a recession.
- The revenue from direct taxation is relatively predictable.

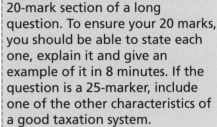

The Canons of Taxation have previously formed the basis for a 20-mark section of a long question. To ensure your 20 marks, you should be able to state each one, explain it and give an example of it in 8 minutes. If the question is a 25-marker, include one of the other characteristics of a good taxation system.

Indirect taxation is a tax on spending. It is collected by the retailer and passed on to the government, e.g. VAT, excise duty, customs duty, stamp duties.

- It tends to be regressive, e.g. the VAT on an item is the same for a person on low income as for a person on high income, thus representing a larger percentage of the poor person's income. However, VAT is higher on luxury goods and zero for many essential goods.
- It doesn't disincentivise work, although it does reduce the spending power of people's income.
- Indirect taxation adds to inflation, making Irish goods less competitive than those purchased abroad.
- The cost of collecting indirect taxes is borne by the retailer, so it is cheap for the government to collect.
- Consumers pay automatically at the point of sale, making it convenient to pay.
- The rates are announced in the Budget each year, and thus follow the principle of certainty.
- The revenue from indirect taxation can fluctuate, e.g. stamp duty on house sales can vary widely.

Tax terms

- A **progressive tax** takes a greater percentage of your income as your income rises, e.g. PAYE.
- A **regressive tax** takes a greater percentage of your income as your income falls, e.g. a TV licence fee of €160 takes a greater percentage of a poor person's income than a rich person's.

Ensure that when you sit your exam, you have a knowledge of the main income tax rates and bands, the VAT rate(s), and the rate of corporation tax.

- **Tax avoidance** means legally reducing your tax bill, e.g. by purchasing a car with lower fuel emissions.
- **Tax evasion** means illegally reducing your tax bill by deliberately under-reporting income.
- **The imposition of a tax**: This refers to the person on whom the tax is officially levied, e.g. a tax on food importers.
- **The incidence of a tax**: This refers to the person who ends up paying the tax, e.g. the food importer adds the tax to the selling price, making the consumer pay it.

The National Debt

The **National Debt** is money borrowed by the government for either current or capital purposes that has not yet been repaid.

- It is made up of **domestic debt** (borrowed from Irish citizens and institutions) and **foreign debt** (borrowed from institutions abroad).
- Ireland's National Debt is managed by the **National Treasury Management Agency (NTMA)**.
- The **Exchequer Borrowing Requirement** is the total borrowed in a year to finance the **current budget deficit** (current expenditure – current revenue) and the **exchequer borrowing requirement for capital purposes** (capital spending – capital revenue).
- The **Public Sector Borrowing Requirement** is the exchequer borrowing requirement plus borrowing for semi-state companies and for local authorities.
- Borrowing helps create economic activity since it represents an injection of money into the economy.
- However, it should be **self-liquidating**, i.e. the economic activity it creates should be generating enough tax revenue to pay back the debt in the long run.
- The size of the National Debt doesn't matter as much as its size as a **ratio of GDP** (National Income), since this tells us more about our ability to afford it. Ireland's National Debt changed little from 1985 to 2007, but our GDP grew hugely, so the National Debt became less of a concern.
- When the 'Celtic Tiger' subsequently ended, tax revenue – particularly stamp duty on new houses – fell sharply. The government borrowed heavily to fund the large current budget deficits that resulted, and to prevent the collapse of the banks. It also began a process of cutting spending, in addition to limited increases in taxation in an attempt to reduce the current budget deficit.
- As a result, a much higher National Debt – along with higher interest payments – has now become a feature of Ireland's public finances and will be for the foreseeable future.
- This means that a higher percentage of tax revenues is needed to pay the interest on the National Debt, and spending in other areas suffers as a result.

It is possible for persistent current budget deficits to drive a country's National Debt so high that a point can be reached when international banks are unwilling to lend a country any more money unless at very high interest rates.

- This is due to a fear of not being repaid if the country defaults on its National Debt. Just like a credit-card limit, a government cannot keep borrowing for ever. Either it stops borrowing at some point, or the lenders stop lending.
- Between 2010 and 2013, the high rates of interest faced by Ireland on international markets required it to avail of emergency loans (a 'bailout') from the IMF, the ECB and the EU (nicknamed 'the Troika').
- These loans carried very strict conditions, involving increases in taxation and sharp reductions in government expenditure in order to quickly reduce the current budget deficit. The government effectively temporarily lost the ability to freely make its own fiscal decisions.
- Ireland emerged from the bailout in 2013 when its national finances recovered sufficiently to cause interest rates on international markets to return to affordable levels.

Ensure that going into the exam, you have up-to-date figures on the size of the National Debt, the ratio of debt to GDP, and the status of Ireland's borrowing capacity.

- Reasons for taxation
- Canons of Taxation
- Progressive and regressive taxes
- Characteristics of direct and indirect taxation
- Tax avoidance and tax evasion
- The imposition of a tax and the incidence of a tax
- How Ireland manages its National Debt

2016, Section B, Question 7 (a)

In the case of the following pairs, distinguish between the two concepts.

 (i) Progressive taxes and regressive taxes

(ii) Impact of taxation and incidence of taxation.

Marking scheme

- Terms correctly distinguished: 10 marks (5 + 5) + 10 marks (5 + 5)
- 20 marks in total

Answer

 (i)

- **Progressive tax:** As income rises, a higher proportion is taken in tax, e.g. The percentage deducted for PAYE rises with income.
- **Regressive tax:** As income rises, a lower proportion is taken in tax, e.g. the VAT on a commodity is the same regardless of the income of the person buying it.

(ii)

- **Impact of taxation:** This is the party on whom the tax is initially imposed, e.g. a tax on imported alcohol.
- **Incidence of taxation:** This is the person who actually ends up paying the tax, e.g. if the tax is passed on to the final consumer.

2014, Section B, Question 8 (a)

Explain the relationship between a government Budget Deficit and the National Debt.

Marking scheme

- 2 definitions @ 10 marks each
- Must explain relationship
- 20 marks in total

Answer

- A budget deficit means that current government spending is greater than current revenue. It must be financed by additional borrowing, which adds to the National Debt.
- The National Debt is the total of outstanding debt borrowed by the government. If there is a budget deficit, it will result in a higher National Debt in addition to higher interest payments.

2014, Section B, Question 8 (c)

Outline possible economic consequences of the Irish Government shifting the burden of taxation from direct taxation to indirect taxation.

Marking scheme

- 4 points @ 5 marks each
- 20 marks in total

Answer

- **Inflation:** Raising indirect taxes increases prices, which may cause consumers to cut or else delay spending.

- **Regressive:** Indirect taxes take a higher proportion of income from those on lower incomes, which would conflict with the principle of equity.

- **Uncertain revenue:** Indirect taxation is less predictable than direct taxation, making it more difficult for the government to plan.

- **Increased investment:** Lower direct taxes on profits would encourage more entrepreneurship and risk-taking.

- **Increased employment:** Lower direct taxes would also allow people to get jobs, engage in overtime and take up promotion since they would be keeping more of their gross pay.

- **Tax evasion:** It is harder to evade indirect taxation since it is it must be paid when purchasing a good or service.

- **Black market:** A move toward indirect taxation may encourage the growth of smuggling in order to avail of lower prices.

20 National Income

aims
- To define National Income
- To outline the three methods for calculating National Income
- To explain the circular flow of income
- To explain the multiplier and how it is calculated

exam focus

This is probably the most examined topic on the Macro part of the course, regularly meriting a full long question. There may be scope to leave *some* Macro topics out, but National Income isn't one of them.

National Income

National Income is the total amount earned by the residents of a country as a result of economic activity in a year.

It can be measured using three different methods:

1. **Income method**: The value of all income earned by the four factors of production is added together.
   - If a factor is provided but no income is actually earned from it, it is not included (e.g. those who work in the home, carers, etc.)
   - **Transfer payments** for which no factor was supplied in exchange are not included, e.g. social welfare payments.
   - **Benefits in kind** (perks) are included, since they represent income in a non-monetary form.
   - **Contributory pensions** are included, because they are payment for past work.
   - **Stock appreciation** is deducted, since it is not actual income but merely inflation.
   - **Financial services**: The excess of interest banks receive on borrowings over the interest they pay on savings is deducted.
   - This gives **Net Domestic Product at Factor Cost**.
   - **Net factor income from the rest of the world** is added. This is the profits of Irish firms located abroad less the profits of foreign firms located here. In the case of Ireland, it is negative.
   - This gives **Net National Income at Factor Cost (National Income)**.

2. **Output method**:
- The total value of everything produced by the agricultural, industrial and services sectors is added together.
  - It is vital to avoid double-counting by including only the value added at each stage.
  - Again, only output for which income is actually earned is included.
- Again, **stock appreciation** and financial services are **deducted**.
- This also gives **Net Domestic Product at Factor Cost**.
- **Net factor income from the rest of the world** is added (negative figure).
- This gives **Net National Income at Factor Cost (National Income)**.
- Depreciation is added.
- This gives **Gross National Product (GNP) at Factor Cost**.
- Indirect taxes (e.g. VAT) are added and government subsidies are deducted.
- The result is **Gross National Product (GNP) at Current Market Prices**.

3. **Expenditure method**:
- The total value of the purchase of goods and services by individuals, firms and government is added together.
  - The purchase of second-hand goods is not included if their original purchase was included in a previous year.
- Exports are added, imports are deducted.
- This gives **Gross Domestic Product at Current Market Prices**.
- **Net Factor Income from the rest of the world** is added (negative figure).
- This also gives an answer called **Gross National Product (GNP) at Current Market Prices**.
- Indierct taxes are deducted and subsidies are added.
- Depreciation is deducted.
- This gives **Net National Income at Factor Cost (National Income)**.

Since we trade with one another constantly, theoretically it shouldn't matter which method is used to measure National Income. Our output is sold in exchange for income, which funds expenditure on the output of others. In reality when collecting such a massive volume of data, however, it is very difficult to avoid statistical discrepancies.

In Ireland, the Central Statistics Office (CSO) uses only the income and expenditure methods, and then gets an average of the two results.

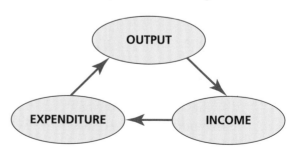

The determinants of National Income

Circular Flow of Income

Payment for the Factors
of Production
- Wages for labour
- Rent for land
- Interest for capital
- Profit for enterprise

FIRMS

HOUSEHOLDS

Purchase of goods and
services

Borrowings/
investment

Earnings from
exports

Government
spending

INJECTIONS

Banks

Foreign markets

Government

Savings

Spending
on imports

Taxation

LEAKAGES

- First, imagine an economy made up of only households and firms. Households sell the four factors of production to firms and in return receive income in the form of wages, rent interest and profit. They then spend this income on the goods and services produced by the firms. The firms use the income from the sale of those goods and services to buy more of the four factors. Again and again, the same money goes around and around in a **circular flow**.

It might appear in the diagram that exports are flowing into the country and imports are flowing out. That is not the case. This diagram refers to the *money spent*, which of course flows the other way. In the exam, you cannot just draw lines, you must draw arrows – and in the correct direction.

- Households may choose not to spend all of their income on goods and services, but to save some of it instead. So now we need to add a **banking sector**.
  - Savings represent a **leakage**, since they're being taken out of the circular flow.
  - On the other hand, others can then borrow that money from the banks and either invest it or spend it. That represents an **injection** into the circular flow.
  - If savings exceed borrowings, there's a reduction in economic activity. GNP falls. If borrowings exceed savings, there's an increase in economic activity. GNP rises.

- Up until now, this was a **closed economy**, i.e. no trade with the outside world. So let's now make it an **open economy**.
  - When we spend money on imported goods and services, this is a **leakage** from the circular flow of income.
  - When Irish goods or services are sold abroad, we experience an **injection** into the circular flow.
  - If imports exceed exports, there's a reduction in economic activity. GNP falls. If exports exceed imports, there's an increase in economic activity. GNP rises.
- Finally, let's give our imaginary country a **government**.
  - When governments collect taxes, that leaves less to be spent on goods and services and hence it's a **leakage**.
  - But governments also spend money in the economy, and that spending represents an **injection**.
  - If taxation exceeds government spending, there's a reduction in economic activity. GNP falls. If government spending exceeds taxation, there's an increase in economic activity. GNP rises.

Therefore, we can think of National Income as being made up of:

- **Consumption**: Income spent on goods and services. It is determined by:
  - Level of income
  - The percentage of income that is spent
- **Investment**: Money borrowed and then spent in the economy. It is determined by:
  - Rate of interest
  - Confidence and expectations of investors
- **Government spending**, e.g. on public sector pay, roads, etc. It is determined by:
  - Political decisions taken by the government
- **Net exports**, i.e. exports − imports
  - Exports are determined by:
    - National income in export markets
    - How competitive our exports are
  - Imports are determined by:
    - Level of income
    - Percentage of income spent on imports

This can also be written as:

$$Y = C + I + G + X - M$$

The circular flow of income and the Multiplier Effect

The size of National Income (Y) will also be affected by the **Multiplier Effect**, i.e. the idea that an initial injection can result in a rise in National Income greater than the initial injection. For example, an injection of €100m, either in the form of government spending or exports or investment, could increase National Income by much more than €100m. Once the initial injection is spent, much of it gets spent *again* by those who receive it, and in turn gets spent again and again each time it comes around in the circular flow. Therefore, National Income can rise by more than the size of the initial injection.

The size of the multiplier – and in turn, National Income – will be affected by:

- **The Marginal Propensity to Consume (MPC)**: The fraction of an increase in income that is spent on goods and services, i.e. that keeps going around the circular flow
- **The Marginal Propensity to Save (MPS)**: The fraction of an increase in income that is saved, and thus leaks out of the circular flow. MPS = 1 − MPC
- **The Marginal Propensity to Import (MPM)**: The fraction of an increase in income that is spent on imports and thus leaks out of the circular flow
- **The Marginal Propensity to pay Tax (MPT)**: The fraction of an increase in income that must be paid to the government in tax, and thus leaks out of the circular flow

Clearly, the larger the MPC is, the larger the multiplier effect will be since that money keeps circulating inside the economy. The higher the MPS, MPM or MPT, the more money that leaks out of the economy and the smaller the multiplier will be.

This can be expressed in the formula:

$$\text{Increase in National Income} = \frac{1}{\text{Leakages}} \times \text{initial injection}$$

For a closed economy with no government, the only leakage is savings. Therefore, the formula will be:

$$\text{Increase in National Income} = \frac{1}{\text{MPS}} \times \text{initial injection}$$

For an open economy with no government, we include the additional leakage caused by imports:

$$\text{Increase in National Income} = \frac{1}{\text{MPS} + \text{MPM}} \times \text{initial injection}$$

Finally, with all three leakages, the formula for an open economy with a government:

$$\text{Increase in National Income} = \frac{1}{\text{MPS} + \text{MPM} + \text{MPT}} \times \text{initial injection}$$

Example:

If you are given a figure of 0.8 for MPC (i.e. consumers spend 80% of their income), you can get MPS simply by subtracting MPC from 1. In this case MPS $= 1 - 0.8 = 0.2$ (i.e. consumers save 20% of their income). With an initial injection of, for example €500m, the increase in National Income for a closed economy with no government sector will be:

$$\frac{1}{0.2} \times €500m = €2,500m$$

If, in addition, the MPM is 0.1 (i.e. consumers spend 10% of their income on imports), the result for an open economy with no government will be:

$$\frac{1}{(0.2 + 0.1)} \times €500m = €1,667m$$

As you would expect, the additional leakage lowers the final addition to National Income.

Finally, if you are told that the MPT is 0.3 (i.e. consumers pay 30% of their income in tax), the answer for an open economy with a government becomes:

$$\frac{1}{(0.2 + 0.1 + 0.3)} \times €500m = €833m$$

Again, the additional leakage makes the result dramatically smaller.

exam focus

Don't be daunted by figures and formulae. Not only do questions on the multiplier appear regularly, but similar questions tend to be repeated. Putting effort into mastering the multiplier is well worth it.

key point

- Definition of National Income
- How National Income is calculated
- $Y = C + I + G + X - M$
- The circular flow of income
- The multiplier and how it is calculated

exam Q

2016, Section B, Question 5 (c)

Explain how Ireland's Gross Domestic Product (GDP) could be affected by any two of the following.

(i) An increase in Child Benefit payments.

(ii) A foreign-owned company, operating in Ireland, sends back to their home country all the profits they have earned in Ireland.

(iii) An oil spill off the Irish coast costs the Irish Government significant clean-up costs.

Marking scheme

- 2 explanations @ 6 marks each
- 2 effects on GDP @ 4 marks each
- 20 marks in total

Answer

(i) An increase in Child Benefit is not included in GDP since it is a transfer payment i.e. no good or service is given in return.

(ii) Since GDP includes all production that takes place in Ireland regardless of where the profit eventually goes, this will have no effect on GDP. It will lower GNP, however.

(iii) Despite the damage to the environment, this will increase GDP because it will involve government spending.

2015, Section B, Question 7 (a)

(i) Explain, with the aid of a diagram, the Circular Flow of Income for an open economy.

(ii) Outline how each of the following should affect the level of National Income in Ireland:

- an increase in Irish exports
- an increase in the level of savings

Marking scheme

- Diagram @ 13 marks
- Explanation @ 10 marks
- Effects @ 6 marks each (3 + 3)
- 35 marks in total

Answer

(i)

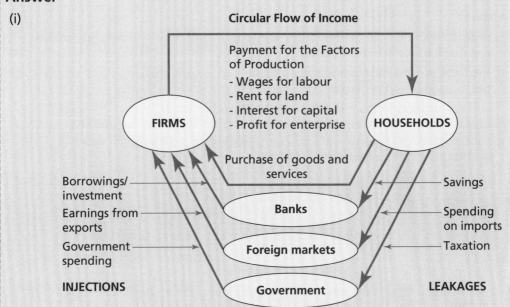

Circular Flow of Income

- **Households** sell the factors production, capital, enterprise, land and labour, to firms in exchange for interest, profit, rent and wages. Using this income, they buy the goods and services that firms produce. In addition, some of their income is saved, some is spent on imports, and some goes in tax to the government.
- **Firms** pay interest, profit, rent and wages to households in exchange for capital, enterprise, land and labour. They use these factors to produce goods and services, which they sell to the households in exchange for payment. In addition, the government will also buy some of their output, banks will invest money in firms, and some of the output will be exported.

(ii)

- **An increase in exports** is an injection into the circular flow. National income will increase by the increase in exports multiplied by the multiplier.
- **An increase in savings** is a leakage from the circular flow. National income will fall by the amount of increased savings multiplied by the multiplier.

2013, Section B, Question 5 (a)

Explain the following terms which are commonly used in estimating the National Income statistics of a country:

- Subsidies
- Incomes-in-kind
- Net Factor Income from the Rest of the World

Marking scheme

- 3 definition @ 5 marks each
- 15 marks in total

Answer

- **Subsidies** are money paid by the state to help a firm keep down the price of the good or service it produces.
- **Incomes-in-kind** is non-monetary income such as private use of a company car, free or subsidised accommodation and preferential loans.
- **Net Factor Income from the Rest of the World** is the difference between income earned by foreign factors of production located in Ireland that is sent abroad and income earned by Irish factors of production located abroad that is returned here to Ireland.

21 ▸ Prices and Inflation

aims
- To define inflation
- To explain how it is measured
- To point out some problems with the CPI
- To outline the uses of the inflation figure
- To discuss the causes and consequences of inflation
- To define deflation and outline its consequences
- To outline ways to combat inflation

Inflation

Inflation is defined as a rise in the general level of prices over a period of time. It reduces the purchasing power of money – if everything goes up in price but you still earn the same, you can no longer buy as much as you could before.

How the government measures inflation:

- A **simple price index** measures the change in price of one product only.
- A **composite price index** measures the change in price of many goods, while also taking into account their relative importance as a share of consumer spending.

- In Ireland, the inflation rate is measured by the Central Statistics Office using the **Consumer Price Index** (CPI). It is drawn up as follows:
  - Every five years, a survey is conducted to establish what the average household spends its income on, and the fraction of income spent on each product.
  - Every month, the prices of each of the thousands of products in the survey are recorded at various places around the country.
  - A base year is chosen, setting all prices in that year = 100. This makes it easier to compare prices in future years.
  - A simple price index is produced for each product. If, after a year, some product has gone up in price by 5%, it is then given a value of 105.
  - A composite price index is conducted by then multiplying each product's value by its weighting.
  - By adding the answers, we get the inflation rate.
  - For example, imagine a simplified world in which there are only three products: milk, bread and apples. Society spends 40% of its income on milk, another 35% on bread, and the last 25% on apples.

Year	Milk	Bread	Apples	CPI
1	$100 \times 40\% = 40$	$100 \times 35\% = 35$	$100 \times 25\% = 25$	100
2	$110 \times 40\% = 44$	$115 \times 35\% = 40.25$	$120 \times 25\% = 30$	114.25
3	$115 \times 40\% = 46$	$125 \times 35\% = 43.75$	$140 \times 25\% = 35$	124.75

  - As you can see, each product's price is set = 100 in Year 1. In Years 2 and 3, as the prices increase, they are given values relative to 100, so that their price can be measured relative to what it was in Year 1.
  - Then they are multiplied by their weightings and the answers are added together to give the CPI for that year. If a simple average was used, a price rise for a product making up a small percentage of spending would be treated the same as a price rise for a more 'important' product.
  - Finally, to calculate the inflation rate, you use the formula:

$$\frac{\text{This year's CPI} - \text{Last year's CPI}}{\text{Last Year's CPI}} \times \frac{100}{1}$$

  - For example, the inflation rate in Year 2 would be:

$$\frac{124.75 - 114.25}{114.25} \times \frac{100}{1} = 9.2\%$$

Some problems with the CPI:

- There is no 'average' household. We have a lot in common, but each of us also buys items few others buy. Rural and urban dwellers, young and old, men and women, and rich and poor all differ in their buying habits. In effect, each of us has our 'own' inflation rate.
- Since households are only surveyed every five years, the CPI loses some of its accuracy since it still uses the weightings from the base year. Old products are still included; new products are not yet included.
- Not all goods are – or can be – included. Only a fixed representative group of goods and services are in the survey.
- As prices rise, consumers switch to cheaper substitute products. This isn't reflected since the weightings are only reassessed every five years. As a result, the inflation rate may be overstated.
- Increases in the quality of goods compensate for price increases, e.g. the average computer processor is continuously improving. The CPI ignores this.
- These problems, however, are prohibitively costly to overcome. So even though the inflation figure is imperfect and frequently criticised, it is still highly useful.

A **Constant Tax Price Index** is one that doesn't include increases in indirect taxes in the CPI.

- Advocates of its use say since people receive services in exchange for the indirect tax increase, they're better off, and so it shouldn't be counted.
- Critics point out that not all people benefit, e.g. if they don't regularly use hospitals, for them the cost of living has gone up.

What is the inflation figure used for?

- Negotiating **wages and social welfare** increases/decreases. If prices are rising, workers will demand higher pay to preserve their cost of living. If they are falling, the government tries to reduce social welfare and public sector pay.
- It can be used as a basis for **widening the tax bands**, since inflation means people are paying more tax even though the tax rate has not changed.

- Measuring international **competitiveness**. If we have a higher inflation rate than our competitors, we export less, and vice versa.
- The Eurozone inflation rate (compiled by Eurostat) is used by the **European Central Bank (ECB)** in deciding whether to adjust interest rates. If inflation is high, the ECB will raise interest rates so as to reduce demand/investment and increase saving, in turn reducing demand-pull inflation (see below). If it is low, the ECB can afford to reduce the interest rate to stimulate the economy. This encourages investment and discourages saving, without much loss of competitiveness.
- It is one of the main **economic indicators**. It reflects the ability of the government and the ECB to control prices.
- It is used in the **indexation of savings**. If the inflation rate is higher than the interest rate, the purchasing power of a person's savings is falling, and they may be discouraged from saving.

Causes of inflation

- **Cost-push** inflation is caused when cost increases are passed on to consumers. This can be due to:
  - A rise in the cost of labour
  - A rise in the cost of raw materials, whether imported or domestically produced
  - A rise in transport or energy costs
- **Demand-pull** inflation happens when supply cannot (or will not) keep up with an increase in demand. Too much money is said to be 'chasing' too few goods. This can be due to:
  - An unexpected increase in consumer confidence
  - Goods that cannot be imported or manufactured fast enough to meet new demand
  - Collusion between firms
  - Firms with monopoly power taking advantage of their position by raising prices
- **Government-caused** inflation is a rise in prices as a result of some action by the government. This can be due to:
  - An increase in indirect taxes, e.g. VAT
  - A decrease in direct taxes, e.g. PAYE can cause demand-pull inflation as people start to spend more
  - An increase in lending by banks due to a lower rate of interest or a relaxation of government lending rules
  - An increase in government expenditure, fuelling demand-pull inflation
  - A rise in interest rates, driving up mortgage costs

Results of inflation

- **Purchasing power of money falls**, e.g. a consumer spending €1000 cannot buy as much as they could with €1000 a year ago. This reduces the standard of living.

- **Unemployment**: If firms cannot pay rising costs, including wages, they may have to lay off workers.
- **Wage-price spiral**: Workers demand higher pay to compensate for inflation, which increases business costs, which are then passed on to consumers. This causes more inflation, feeding more wage demands, and the spiral continues.
- The **uncertainty** that this causes is not a good climate for investment, where any risk is unhelpful.
- **Loss of competitiveness**: If inflation is higher in Ireland than abroad, it becomes harder to export goods. In addition, more Irish people try to shop abroad. As exports fall and imports rise, jobs may be lost.
- A **rise in government spending**: As costs to the government go up, it has to spend more to get the same.
- **Speculation** is encouraged: Money is falling in value, so people switch to assets that might hold their value, e.g. wine, art or land.
- Those on **fixed incomes suffer** most. Social welfare and state pensions are adjusted only once a year in the Budget, but workers could get their pay increased more quickly.
- A **rise in interest rates**: If the Eurozone inflation rate is too high, the **ECB** will raise interest rates to combat it.
- If the **inflation rate exceeds the interest rate**, there's a negative **real interest rate** (nominal or published rate – inflation rate), which reduces purchasing power. It becomes very cheap to borrow and there is an incentive to spend rather than save.

How to reduce inflation

- **Increase the interest rate**. This is a power Ireland handed over to the ECB when we joined the Euro. Their focus is on the Eurozone inflation rate, not just Ireland's. Therefore:
  - If Ireland has low inflation but the Eurozone has high inflation, Ireland will get a higher interest rate than we'd prefer, curtailing economic growth.
  - If Ireland has high inflation and the Eurozone has low inflation, Ireland will get a lower interest rate than we'd prefer, leading to further inflation and possibly causing economic 'overheating'.
- In order to fight inflation ourselves, we must resort to **fiscal policy** and other measures that take money out of the economy, reducing demand and therefore reducing inflation:
  - **Indirect taxes** (e.g. VAT) may be increased so as to lower demand, but if demand is inelastic, they may instead add to inflation. In that case, it's better to reduce them.
  - **Direct taxes** (e.g. PAYE) can be used to take money out of people's pockets and thus reduce demand-pull inflation.
  - A **saving scheme** encourages saving and takes money out of the economy.

- Lower **government spending**: The government is the economy's biggest consumer. If it buys less, inflation can be reduced. This can be politically difficult.
- **National wage agreements** between the main employers' representatives, the unions and the government (the 'social partners') make wage increases more predictable and thus can help to control inflation.
- **Bank regulation**: By making it harder to get loans, the Central Bank can reduce demand, and hence inflation too.
- **Competition**: More competition in the market can help to keep prices low by giving consumers more products to choose from.

As you can see, measures to fight inflation may also cost jobs. This trade-off was also covered in Chapter 18.

Deflation

Deflation is negative inflation – prices are going down rather than up. It can be caused by:

- **Over-supply** relative to demand, e.g. more hotel rooms than there are people to stay in them.
- **Repeated government surpluses** taking money out of the economy, i.e. government taxation greater than spending.
- **Persistent unfavourable balance of payments** – more money leaving the country on imports than coming in on exports.
- A **sudden drop** in demand or investment or government spending or all three, e.g. in a recession.

Results of deflation

- An increase in the **purchasing power of money**. Employers use this to justify wage cuts and the government uses it to justify cuts in social welfare.
- **Deflationary spiral**: Lower prices lead to lower wages, which lead to lower prices. The expectation that this will continue can lead to a fall in demand as people wait for prices to fall even further. In this way, deflation can be just as bad as inflation.
- The government saves money on **capital projects** as the cost of construction and raw materials falls, e.g. it costs less to build a motorway than it did before.

- **Increased national competitiveness**, provided Irish prices fall by more than competing countries' prices do.
- Higher **real interest rates** encourage people to save more and borrow less. This reduces demand, investment and employment.
- The **rate of defaults** on loans (people unable to repay) rises and the value of collateral (security) falls.
- Those on **fixed incomes** gain since it's politically difficult to cut their payments, e.g. old-age pensions.

Again, when you see lists like these, start to think of possible exam questions and marking schemes: 20-markers, 25-markers, 30-markers.

- Definition of inflation
- How inflation is measured
- Problems with the CPI
- Uses of the inflation figure
- Causes and consequences of inflation
- Definition of deflation
- Consequences of deflation
- Measures government can take to eliminate inflation

2015, Section B, Question 6 (a)

(i) Do you consider the CPI an accurate measure of changes in the cost of living? Explain your answer.

(ii) Discuss two possible economic effects of price deflation on the Irish economy.

Marking scheme
- Correct answer @ 2 marks
- 3 reasons @ 5 marks each
- 2 effects of deflation @ 4 marks each
- 25 marks in total

Answer

(i) No, the CPI is not an accurate measure of changes in the cost of living, for the following reasons:

- **New products:** As long as the index is not updated with new products, it inevitably lags behind how the public spends its money.
- **Dangers of the average:** The CPI is based on average spending patterns for the population in general, and hence may be unrepresentative of many if not most people's spending.
- **Cost of living:** The CPI only addresses price changes, but changes in tax and welfare rates also affect people's cost of living.
- **Switch to cheaper substitutes:** People respond to price rises by switching to cheaper alternatives, which is not reflected in the CPI.
- **Urban versus rural:** Differences in the rate of inflation in town and country, due to the different goods and services purchased, are not reflected in the CPI.
- **Product quality:** The index does not reflect improvements in the quality of products, which can more than compensate for any price increases and sometimes don't involve price increases at all, e.g. vast improvements in information technology.
- **Base year weights:** The CPI uses the weights devised in the base year, but as these change over time the CPI loses some of its accuracy.

(ii)

- **More competitive:** Falling prices make our exports more attractive.
- Increased debt burden: Since the nominal value of loan repayments doesn't change, but the purchasing power of the money is now higher due to lower prices, the real value of the debt effectively increases.
- **More purchasing power:** As prices fall, the amount that can be purchased with a given amount of money rises, thus increasing its purchasing power.
- **Decline in aggregate demand:** In anticipation of further prices decreases, consumers postpone their purchases.
- **Fall in investment:** Due to the fall in consumer demand, in anticipation of further falls in the price of capital goods, investors also delay their investment decisions.
- **Vicious spiral:** Deflation can create a vicious circle of falling demand and investment, falling profits, higher unemployment and more defaults on loans.

2013, Section B, Question 6 (ii)

Outline two uses of the CPI, other than as a measure of the rate of inflation.

Marking scheme
- 2 marks @ 5 marks each
- 10 marks in total

Answer
- **Major economic indicator:** CPI statistics, along with economic growth, unemployment etc., is an important indicator of Ireland's overall economic performance.
- **Pay negotiations:** Trade unions tend to use inflation figures as a justification for higher pay claims.
- **Indexation of savings and investments:** Savings and investment products often 'index-link' their rate of return to the rate of inflation.
- **Indexation of tax bands and social welfare payments:** If tax bands and thresholds are not increased in line with inflation, the net gain from a tax cut is reduced because inflation reduces its purchasing power. Conversely, because deflation increases the purchasing power of money, the government may argue that it can cut social welfare without cutting the standard of living.
- **International competitiveness:** If inflation here is greater than it is in other countries, our exports lose competitiveness and vice versa.

- To define money
- To set out the functions and characteristics of money
- To explain how banks 'create' money
- To explain the limitations on banks' ability to create money
- To explain liquidity and profitability, and the Money Supply
- To explain the role of the European Central Bank (ECB)
- To explain exchange rates and the factors that affect them
- To explain the role of the International Monetary Fund (IMF), the World Bank, and the European Investment Bank (EIB)

The banking industry is of critical importance in our society, since it provides the means for investors to borrow based on the savings of others, thus facilitating the creation of capital and the expansion of the economy. Since the rest of the economy depends on it working properly, the banking industry needs to be carefully monitored and regulated by the government.

Money

Before we can talk about banking, we must first define money:

- **Money** is anything that is generally accepted as a way of paying for goods and services.
- Shells, cigarettes, cattle and particularly gold have been used as money at various times. These gave way to notes and coins.
- More recently, we have begun to use cheques, credit cards and now computerised transactions. These are called **near money**.

- **Token money** is money whose intrinsic value is less than its face value, e.g. a €500 note costs less than a Euro to print, yet an airline will fly you all the way to New York and back in exchange for it. In the past, currency was often backed by gold, meaning that you could cash in a £10 note for £10 worth of gold. Money not backed by gold is also called **fiat money** or **fiduciary issue**, since it is based on trust.
- The crucial feature all money has in common is that as long as enough people *accept* it as payment, then it is money.
- The official currency in Ireland is the Euro. By law it must be accepted in payment, i.e. it is **legal tender**. Cheques and credit cards are not legal tender.
- Money replaced the practice of **barter** (or **counter-trade**), which involved swapping things.
- If one person had a horse and another had a cow, they might agree to swap.
- Barter depended on, among other things, a **double coincidence of wants** – each party had to want what the other was offering.
- This happened quite frequently in traditional societies, but as goods and services became more numerous, and people's needs became more varied, it became less likely.
- A new system was required – money.

Money performs **four** main functions:

1. **Medium of exchange**: Money makes swapping unnecessary, since you can sell your cow to one person, and then later use the money to buy a horse from someone else. It avoids the need for the double coincidence of wants, and thus makes buying and selling much more flexible.

2. **Unit of account**: Money allows all goods and services to be compared in terms of value on the same scale, e.g. a €13 haircut is worth half as much as a €26 umbrella. It provides a common denominator. This is something that wasn't possible with barter, e.g. what if a cow and a horse weren't considered to be of equal value?

3. **Standard of deferred payment**: Money enables the purchase of goods on credit (buy now, pay later). Under barter, people were reluctant to trade on credit since they didn't know their future needs. With money, whatever your future needs, you can use money to pay for them. This makes trade far more flexible, allowing consumers to pay for expensive items such as cars over a long period of time.

4. **Store of wealth**: Money allows people to save in order to pay for future transactions. This is harder to do under barter since goods that are traded are perishable. Another advantage is that when people save money, it allows others to borrow that money through the banking system and invest it.

> These four functions can form the basis for a nice 20-mark question – four functions at 5 marks each. Every time you see a list, try to think of it in terms of a potential question and its marking scheme.

Money also should have some other characteristics:

- **Acceptable**: Money stops being money if it's no longer accepted. People should have **confidence** that the money they have will be accepted, otherwise trade will break down.
- **Scarce**: It should be scarce in relation to the demand for it. Otherwise it lacks value.
- **Homogenous**: Each denomination of it should be identical, e.g. one €20 note and another €20 note.
- **Portable**: It should be easy to carry around. Small amounts of notes and coins don't weigh much, cows do.
- **Durable**: It should last a long time, e.g. coins are made of metal and notes are made of cotton fibre.
- **Recognisable**: People should not have to question whether they've been handed real money. This is why so much effort is put into stopping counterfeiting (the making of fake money). Again, this preserves **confidence**.
- **Divisible**: It must come in small as well as large denominations, not just €500 notes but also 5c coins for smaller transactions.

How does banking work?

- When gold was used as money, people deposited it with goldsmiths to keep it secure. The goldsmiths issued them with receipts.
- Since these receipts could be exchanged for gold, they themselves became accepted as payment. They were the first bank notes and the goldsmiths were the first banks.
- The goldsmiths soon realised that once people made deposits with them, they could lend out receipts to people who needed to borrow money, and charge them interest on it.
- But what about the fact that there were now more receipts than there was gold? The goldsmiths quickly discovered that this wasn't a problem, since on any given day, only a small fraction of the receipts were submitted in exchange for gold. In this way, banks could 'create' money.
- Eventually, the government started to issue official currency in place of the receipts. This was the beginning of legal tender.
- Later, it was realised that there was no need for gold at all. As long as people accept the notes (and coins), it doesn't have to be backed by anything except people's belief that it will be accepted.
- Banks still do this today. Just like the goldsmith issuing a receipt for gold that he doesn't have, loans today are issued for cash the bank doesn't have and doesn't need to have – since only a small fraction of savers want their money in cash on any given day.
- For example:
  - Gráinne lodges €100 in cash to her account.
  - The bank lends €900 to Kevin, not in the form of cash – because the only cash it has is Gráinne's €100 – but in the form of a bank account with €900 in it.

- Before we had only €100, now we have €1,000.
- Since there's only about a 10% chance that Gráinne or Kevin will wish to withdraw their money in cash on any given day, the bank only needs Gráinne's original €100 to cover both accounts, *not* the €1,000 that's now in them.
- The bank has thus 'created' an extra €900.
- The number of times the cash deposit can be lent out in the form of loans is called the reserve ratio.
- Increase in credit = (Increase in Cash Deposits × Reserve Ratio).

How banks do this is puzzling at first, so it requires repeated study. It's not a magic trick, it simply depends on keeping only enough money 'in stock' to satisfy demand on any particular day. When you think about it, isn't this what shops do with bread, shoes, petrol and everything else anyway? Money is in some ways just another product, subject to the laws of supply and demand – and stock management.

- It depends on trust – as long as borrowers believe they must pay their debts, and as long as savers believe their deposits are safe, the system works quite well. To preserve this trust, banks need to be carefully regulated to ensure they are run with the utmost integrity.
- A **run on the banks** happens if savers all try to withdraw their money and can't.
- Banks act as a medium that allows money to flow from savers to borrowers without those two people having to meet.
- When banks create money, it boosts consumer demand but can also add to inflation.

Limitations on the power of a bank to create money

- **The primary liquidity ratio**: The ratio of cash a bank must by law hold to cover total deposits, e.g. a ratio of 10% means it must have €10 in cash for every €100 on deposit (the €10 itself, plus the €90 it was used to create).
- **The secondary liquidity ratio**: The ratio of exchequer bills and government bonds a bank must by law have to cover total deposits, e.g. a ratio of 25% means it must have €25 in liquid assets to cover every €100 of deposits.
- **Depositors**: Banks need depositors in order to have borrowers, and must offer sufficient interest rates to attract them, e.g. if the primary liquidity ratio is 10%, a bank cannot lend €900 if it only has €50 on deposit.
- **Suitable borrowers**: The primary liquidity ratio might be 10%, but just because a bank has €100 in cash doesn't mean it has a loan applicant capable of repaying a €900 loan. When banks run out of suitable borrowers, they start to lend to unsuitable borrowers. Following the end of the 'Celtic Tiger', the Irish banks suffered heavy losses due to the collapse of the housing market and the bad debts that resulted from housing developers going bankrupt. As a result, the Irish government set up NAMA

(see Chapter 14), nationalised much of the banking industry and pumped billions of Euro in additional funds into the Irish banks to prevent their collapse.

- In addition to the liquidity ratios, the **ECB** – which is charged with the task of limiting inflation – has wide powers to limit credit creation:
  - **The rediscount rate**: This is the rate the ECB charges when it lends to the banks. The higher this is, the less they can borrow, and the less they can lend. The rediscount rate dictates all other interest rates.
  - **Open market operations**: The ECB can sell shares or securities on the stock exchange. The buyers pay for them by writing cheques, which the ECB then cashes. This withdrawal of cash restricts the banks' lending capacity. The ECB can also buy shares in order to do the opposite.
  - **Supplementary deposits**: The ECB can force banks to deposit with it, giving them less scope to lend.
  - **Statements and opinions on the economy:** When the ECB comments on the economy or hints at future actions, this can influence expectations in the market.

Liquidity and profitability

- Banks want to make profits for their shareholders, but are restricted by their requirement to hold cash, thus limiting their profitability in order to preserve their liquidity.
- The more liquid the asset a bank holds, the less profitable and vice versa.
- In order of decreasing liquidity, a bank's assets are: cash, money on call (at short notice), exchequer bills, government bonds (gilt-edged securities), term loans and overdrafts.

The Money Supply, as defined by the ECB:

- **M1 (narrow money supply)**: Currency, i.e. notes and coins, plus balances that can immediately be changed into currency or used for cashless payments, i.e. overnight deposits
- **M2 (intermediate money supply)**: M1 + deposits with an agreed maturity up to two years and deposits redeemable at a period of notice up to three months
- **M3 (broad money supply)**: M2 + repurchase agreements + money market fund shares/units + debt securities up to two years

The exchange rate

The **exchange rate** is the price of one currency in terms of another. It is determined by:

- **Balance of payments**: If a country exports more than it imports, foreigners will need to buy the currency to pay for their purchases, driving up its value in the process.

- **Interest rates**: If interest rates are high in a country, money will obviously flow into its banks, creating a demand for its currency and driving up its value.
- **Speculation**: People are constantly betting on currencies by buying them today in the hope they can sell them tomorrow at a profit. This activity affects their value.
- **Actions of the ECB**: If the value of the Euro is falling, the ECB buys it up, thereby reducing its supply and driving up its value.
- **Fiscal policy**: A country that puts more money in the hands of its citizens risks creating a demand for exports that can weaken the value of its currency.
- **Purchasing Power Parity (PPP)**: In a free market, the exchange rate should in theory settle at a level where a given amount of a currency will have the same purchasing power wherever it is spent. In practice, it doesn't.
- **Devaluation**: When the value of a currency is deliberately lowered in order to correct a balance of payments deficit. It can cause inflation as imported raw materials are now more expensive. **Revaluation** is the opposite of devaluation.

Types of exchange rates

- A **fixed (pegged) exchange rate** means a currency is matched to the value of another currency or a basket of currencies.
  - It encourages trade by eliminating exchange risk.
  - It gets rid of speculation.
  - The government has to constantly buy or sell its own currency to keep the desired value, and has to maintain reserves of foreign currency for this reason.
- A **floating exchange** rate means that market conditions (supply and demand) are allowed to determine the exchange rate of a currency.
  - It reduces the need for the government to intervene in the currency market or to maintain large reserves.
  - The Balance of payments' surpluses and deficits are automatically corrected, i.e. if a country has a deficit, its currency should fall in value, bringing exports and imports back into agreement.
  - It creates greater exchange rate uncertainty, which discourages trade and investment.
  - It is common to let a currency float between an upper and a lower limit. This is called a **managed float**.

The ECB and the ESCB

Since Ireland joined the Euro, the **Irish Central Bank** is part of the **European System of Central Banks (ESCB)**, which also comprises the European Central Bank.

You will see the ECB mentioned again and again throughout the Macro section of this book. Even though you might not have heard of it before, it plays a crucial role in the economic life of our country.

- The ECB decides Eurozone **monetary policy**, i.e. it controls the money supply by means of the interest rate, with the objective of achieving price stability and stable economic growth.
- The tools it uses to achieve this are:
  - **Main refinancing operations (MROs)**: Open market operations to lend money (liquidity) to the banks. The rate charged influences commercial interest rates.
  - **The marginal lending facility**: This allows banks to draw down overnight liquidity. The interest rate charged sets the upper limit for the overnight market interest rate.
  - **The deposit facility**: This allows banks to make overnight deposits with the ECB. The rate earned sets the lower limit for the overnight market interest rate.
  - **Minimum reserve requirements**: The ECB forces Irish banks to make minimum deposits with the Irish Central Bank.

The ECB is made up of three components:

- **Executive Board** (President, Vice-President and 4 appointees)
- **General Council** (Executive Board + Governors of all EU national central banks)
- **Governing Council** (Executive Board + Governors of all Eurozone national central banks)

Functions of the Irish Central Bank (as part of the ESCB)

- Represent Ireland on the Governing Council of the ECB
- Implement ECB monetary policy in Ireland
- Supply Ireland's share of the Euro notes and coins
- Manage Ireland's official external currency reserves
- Supervise the Irish credit institutions
- Publish research in its quarterly reports
- Act as the Irish government's bank
- Be answerable to the Oireachtas

Other international economic institutions

- **The IMF** was set up in 1945 in order to:
  - Oversee the global financial system, particularly in relation to exchange rates and the balance of payments
  - Advise member countries on their economic policies
  - Provide emergency loans to countries in financial crisis which can no longer borrow to fund themselves. Such loans carry strict conditions, including tax increases and severe spending cuts in order to balance the budget. (See also Chapter 19)
  - Provide cheap loans to poorer member countries
  - Promote international trade and economic growth
- **The World Bank** was set up in 1944 to:
  - Provide loans to **Less Developed Countries (LDCs)** for capital projects, e.g. roads, irrigation
  - Reduce poverty and eradicate hunger
- **The European Investment Bank (EIB)** was set up in 1958 to:
  - Finance capital projects that further EU objectives
  - Promote development in poorer areas of the EU
  - Encourage EU economic integration

key point

- Money and its origins
- The functions and characteristics of money
- How banks create money
- The competing aims of liquidity and profitability
- The money supply and how the ECB controls it
- Exchange rates and the factors that affect them
- Economic institutions and their roles

2015, Section B, Question 5 (a)
 (i) Outline three factors that limit the ability of banks to create credit.
(ii) Discuss the economic reasons why the financial system in Ireland should be regulated.

Marking scheme

- 3 factors @ 6 marks each (3 + 3)
- 2 reasons @ 6 marks each (3 + 3)
- 30 marks in total

Answer

 (i) 3 factors that limit the ability of banks to create credit:

- **Availability of creditworthy borrowers:** A bank may have a large amount of cash deposits, but it can only create credit if it attracts enough suitable borrowers.
- **Scale of cash deposits:** On the other hand, a bank may have willing and creditworthy customers eager to take out loans, but it's ability to do so is still constrained by the amount of cash it must hold to meet the demands of depositors. If depositors demand more cash, the bank's power to extend loans is reduced accordingly.
- **Demand for loans:** Even creditworthy customers won't borrow money if they are wary of the risks of doing so, e.g. due to economic uncertainty. Investor confidence is a major factor in the demand for loans.
- **The European Central Bank Bank (ECB):** The ECB can reduce the ability of the banks to offer credit in several ways, e.g. by issuing regulations, changing the bank rate, adjusting the required capital ratios or the reserve requirement.

(ii) Economic reasons why the financial system in Ireland should be regulated:

- **To prevent reckless lending:** Tempted by high profits in the short-term, the Irish banks have in the past been guilty of lending too much money to borrowers who could not repay it, thus incurring huge losses that were eventually absorbed by the taxpayer. Regulation is required to prevent this from happening again.
- **To protect depositors:** When the public trust the banks with their deposits, they deserve to know that their savings will be kept safe. This also requires careful regulation.
- **To counter the boom-bust cycle:** Unregulated profit-seeking banks may lend too much when the economy is growing and little or nothing at all when it is shrinking, thus adding to the worst aspects both of booms and of busts. Regulation may help to create more stable and sustainable growth.
- **To maintain public confidence:** A stable financial system depends on the public believing that their money is secure and that banks are prudently managed and properly monitored.

2013, Section B, Question 6 (a) (i)
Explain, using a numerical example, how banks create credit in an economy.

Marking scheme
Option A
- Explanation: 4 points @ 4 marks each
- 4 points for numerical example (1 mark for each asterisked* figure)

Option B
- 4 marks for balance sheet credit is created
- 6 marks for balance sheet after credit is created
- Explanation: 5 points @ 2 marks each
- 20 marks in total

Answer
Option A
- €100 in cash is deposited at a bank.
- The bank knows from experience that there is only a 10% chance that this cash will be withdrawn on any given day. The bank sets aside €10 in cash for this purpose.
- That leaves €90 to lend to other customers, but they are also subject to the 10% ratio, so therefore it is possible to lend them $900.
- Increase in credit = Increase in Cash Deposits × $\dfrac{1}{\text{Reserve Ratio}}$

Numerical example
A person deposits €100 at a bank. The bank's reserve ratio is 10%. The bank can create credit as follows:

$$€100 \times \frac{1}{10\%} = €1000 \; [-€100 = €900]$$

Option B

Bank's Balance Sheet before credit is created

Assets	€	Liabilities	€
Cash lodged by Mairead	100	Mairead's deposit	100
Total assets	100	Total liabilities	100

Bank's Balance Sheet after credit is created

Assets	€	Liabilities	€
Cash lodged by Mairead	100	Mairead's deposit	100
Loans	900	New deposits	900
Total assets	1000	Total liabilities	1000

Explanation

- €100 is lodged to the bank.
- The bank knows that only 10% will be demanded in cash.
- It therefore has enough cash to support total deposits of €1000.
- The bank can 'create' another €900 in deposits. It does this by giving out loans of €900.

23 Trade

aims
- To define trade and different types of trade
- To explain the balance of trade and the balance of payments
- To explain the Terms of Trade
- To describe the benefits of international trade
- To set out the Law of Absolute Advantage
- To set out the Law of Comparative Advantage
- To outline the limitations of the Law of Comparative Advantage
- To outline the justifications for restricting trade
- To describe the methods used to restrict trade
- To outline the role of the World Trade Organization (WTO)

exam focus

Trade is one of the most regular Macro topics, appearing almost as often as National Income and the multiplier.

Trade

Trade with other countries involves exports and imports:

- **Visible exports**: Goods sold to foreigners by Irish firms, e.g. pharmaceutical drugs manufactured in Mayo sold to the US
- **Invisible exports**: Services sold to foreigners by Irish firms, e.g. a French tourist stays in a Killarney hotel
- **Visible imports**: Goods bought by Irish people from foreign firms, e.g. a South Korean mobile phone sold in Longford
- **Invisible imports**: Services bought by Irish people from foreign firms, e.g. an Austrian orchestra gives a concert in Dublin
- **Balance of trade**: Visible exports – visible imports
  - If exports exceed imports, it is **favourable**.
  - If imports exceed exports, it is **unfavourable**.

The balance of payments in composed of two parts:

- **Balance of payments on current account (day-to-day)**: (Visible + invisible exports) − (visible + invisible imports)
  - If it is in deficit, it means more money is leaving the country than coming in, costing jobs. In the SR, this can be financed by borrowing.
  - However, in the LR, a country must pay for its imports by exporting – just like a household must work to pay for what it consumes.
  - A deficit can be reduced by:
    - **Increasing exports**, e.g. by paying subsidies
    - **Decreasing imports**, using tariffs, etc.
    - **Devaluation of the currency,** making exports cheaper abroad and imports dearer here. Since we joined the Euro, Ireland cannot devalue on its own; only the Eurozone can.

- **Balance of payments on capital account**:
  - A record of receipts and payments on capital (one-off) transactions.
    - **Receipts**: Government borrowing, foreign purchases of Irish shares or property, foreign firms investing here, EU grants.
    - **Payments**: Irish people buying shares or property abroad (e.g. Spain), Irish firms investing abroad.

The Terms of Trade are an indicator of how much is imported per export:

$$\text{Terms of Trade} = \frac{\text{Index of Export Prices}}{\text{Index of Import Prices}} \times 100$$

- If it improves, Ireland has to export less to import the same quantity as before:
  - This is called a **'favourable movement'**.
  - It happens if export prices rise relative to import prices:
    - If both rise, but export prices rise more
    - If both fall, but export prices fall less
    - If export prices rise and import prices don't change
    - If import prices fall and export prices don't change
- If it worsens, Ireland has to export more to import the same quantity as before:
  - This is called an **'unfavourable movement'**.
  - It happens if import prices rise relative to export prices:
    - If both rise, but import prices rise more
    - If both fall, but import prices fall less
    - If import prices rise and export prices don't change
    - If export prices fall and import prices don't change

Benefits of international trade

- **Wider choice of goods**: A small country such as Ireland can import goods, services and raw materials not available at home.

- **Bigger markets**: By exporting, a firm benefits from economies of scale, allowing it to cut prices both at home and abroad. This boosts exports further while benefiting domestic consumers too.

- **Employment and investment**: Exporting creates jobs in the home economy. Firms invest in order to meet demand.

- **Standard of living**: Exports increase National Income, thus improving the standard of living.

- **Foreign currency**: Exports earn foreign currency needed to pay for imports. A balance of payments surplus also increases the value of the Euro.

- **Competition**: Domestic firms must cut costs and prices if they are to stand up to international competition, benefiting domestic consumers.

- **Multinational companies**: Free trade allows them to spread production worldwide, benefiting from economies of scale. Lower prices are passed on to consumers. Unfortunately, oligopolies also emerge.

- **Market for excess output**: Once a country has provided for its own needs, it can export excess output to others who need it, and vice versa, e.g. Ireland exports most of the medical devices produced here.

> Since in economic terms a country is just a group of people, keep in mind that the benefits of trade can apply to any other group of people – a city, a county, even an individual. We all need to trade.

- **Better international relations**: When countries trade, contact and mutual understanding is increased, and the potential for conflict reduced.

- **Economic recovery**: Whenever the domestic economy is in recession, exports can help it to recover.

The laws of absolute and comparative advantage

The law of absolute advantage (Adam Smith)

By specialising in the production of the good in which it has an absolute advantage, and obtaining its other needs from international trade, each country gains.

- To explain, imagine that there are only two countries, Ireland and Germany. Each country has only two workers – one makes clothes, the other grows food. Initially the two countries **do not** trade with one another.

- Ireland is able to produce more clothes than Germany, giving Ireland an **absolute advantage** in the production of clothes (80 compared to 50).

- Similarly, Germany has an absolute advantage in the production of food (100 compared to 50).

Production before trade

	Food	Clothes
Ireland	50	80
Germany	100	50
Total	150	130

- If each country specialises in the production of that good in which it has an absolute advantage (i.e. if it assigns *both* of its workers to the production of that good instead of only one), we get the following result:

- When they each produce what they are better at, and buy the other good from their neighbour, the total food produced increases from 150 to 200 units, and the production of clothing grows from 130 units to 160.

Production after trade

	Food	Clothes
Ireland	0	160
England	200	0
Total	200	160

- Both countries have gained from trade.

The law of comparative advantage (David Ricardo)

By specialising in the production of the good in which it is **relatively more efficient,** and obtaining its other needs from international trade, each country gains.

- This means that even if one of the countries has an absolute advantage over the other in the production of **both** food **and** clothes, it is still possible for both to gain from specialisation and trade.

Production before trade

	Food	Clothes
Ireland	50	40
Germany	100	60
Total	150	100

- England has an absolute advantage in the production of both goods (100 compared to 50, 60 compared to 40).

- But while a German worker is twice as efficient as an Irish worker at producing food, a German worker is only one and a half times as efficient as an Irish worker at producing clothing.

- Therefore, Germany has a **comparative advantage** in the production of food, i.e. it is **relatively more efficient** at producing food than at producing clothing.

- Similarly, Ireland is only half as good as Germany at food production, but two thirds as good as Germany at clothing production.

- Therefore, Ireland has a **comparative advantage** in the production of clothing, i.e. Ireland is **relatively more efficient** at producing clothing than at producing food.

- If Germany specialises in food and Ireland specialises in clothing, we get the following:

- Food production has risen from 150 to 200 units.

- But clothing production has *fallen* from 100 to 80 units.

Production after trade

	Food	Clothes
Ireland	0	80
Germany	200	0
Total	200	80

- We must ask: Is the gain of 50 units of food enough to compensate for the loss of 20 units of clothing?

- The totals *before* trade were 150 units of food and 100 units of clothing, i.e. 1 unit of clothing is equal to 1.5 units of food.

- This ratio suggests that if we had to, we would be willing to give up as much as 33.3 units of clothing to gain 50 extra units of food.

- But – by specialisation and trading – we gain 50 units of food but only give up *20* units of clothing.

- Therefore, we still gain from trade even when one country enjoys an absolute advantage in the production of *both* goods.

The above explanation requires repeated step-by-step study. It also helps to make up your own figures and realise the gains for yourself.

- By way of analogy, picture a lawyer who is five times better at being a lawyer than her secretary and one and a half times better at typing than her secretary. It makes better sense for the lawyer to do the lawyering and the secretary to do the typing rather than the lawyer to do both and the secretary to do nothing.

Terms of Trade:

Ireland:

- 1 unit of food is equal to 0.8 units of clothing
- 1 unit of clothing is equal to 1.25 units of food

Germany:

- 1 unit of food is equal to 0.6 units of clothing
- 1 unit of clothing is equal to 1.67 units of food

Possible terms of trade:

- Food lies between 0.6 and 0.8 units of clothing
- Clothing lies between 1.25 and 1.67 units of food

Problems with the law of comparative advantage

- **Constant returns to scale**: It is assumed that two workers can produce twice as much food as one. This ignores the Law of Diminishing Marginal Returns.

- **Transport costs ignored**: The gains from specialisation can be cancelled out or even exceeded by the transport costs between the countries.
- **Free trade restrictions**: Governments frequently interfere in trade, reducing the gains that can be made.
- **Occupationally mobility**: It is implied that you can be a baker today and a tailor tomorrow. In reality, lengthy retraining is often needed.
- **Strategic reasons for avoiding specialisation**: Countries might prefer to diversify their production rather than depend on others for vital imports, or depend on a single export for their income.

Trade restrictions

Despite the advantages of international trade, in response to domestic lobbying, governments frequently try to **restrict** it. This is called **protectionism**. A number of justifications are frequently used:

- To protect **employment**: The government may wish to block imports of goods that could be produced in Ireland, thus creating jobs here instead of abroad.
- To protect from competition in **low-wage countries**.
- **Balance of payments deficit**: If imports consistently exceed exports, the government may wish to impose barriers in order to restore the balance.
- Protection against **dumping**, i.e. a foreign firm attempting to enter the Irish market by selling here below the price it charges at home or below cost.
- **Infant industries**: To allow small firms to gain economies of scale so that they can compete internationally. The barriers are then supposed to be lifted, but this is frequently postponed.
- To allow **phasing out** of an industry: If an industry is dying, rather than letting it collapse, the government may opt to phase out restrictions, giving workers time to find alternative employment.
- To reduce dependence on imports of **vital goods**. This avoids scarcity of important goods, e.g. oil. It also reduces shortages during war.
- To achieve **political aims**. Trade barriers are used as a means of political pressure e.g. UN sanctions against Syria. The leaders are the intended target but often the ordinary citizens suffer most, e.g. medicine shortages.
- **Retaliation** against another country for imposing trade restrictions on your exports to it.

Barriers to trade have several negative effects:

- They erode the **gains from trade** already outlined.
- They restrict **consumer choice** and freedom.
- They increase the cost of imported **raw materials**.
- They insulate **inefficient producers** from the realities of international competition.
- They foster a **dependence on continued protection** that leaves producers even less prepared for when the barriers are eventually removed.

How governments interfere in international trade

- **Tariffs**: Taxes on imports that raise the price of imports. They are also a source of government revenue.
- **Quotas**: A limit on the amount that can be imported, leaving the rest of the market to domestic firms.
- **Subsidies**: Government payments to domestic producers to help them compete with foreign competitors.
- **Exchange controls**: Imports from a particular country are limited to a specified money value, e.g. €3 billion.
- **Administrative barriers**: Paperwork, 'red tape', regulations, etc. that are solely intended to discourage the importation of goods, e.g. time-consuming, costly and needless form-filling.
- **Embargo**: This is a ban on a foreign country's imports or a ban on exports to that nation or both, e.g. US embargo on Cuba. It can also mean a ban on a specified good regardless of the country of origin, e.g. illegal drugs.

The WTO

The World Trade Organisation (WTO) is an international body – of which Ireland is a member – that aims to reduce trade barriers and promote international trade.

- It provides a forum for negotiations (called 'rounds').
- Ireland is represented at these negotiations by the EU.
- It settles trade disputes.
- **'Most Favoured Nation' clause**: If you lift trade barriers for one country, you must lift them for all.
- The WTO has successfully negotiated dramatic falls in trade barriers and an expansion in world trade, but it still has more to do.
- Critics of free trade argue that it exploits the poor, destroys local cultures, creates powerful global oligopolies, and results in an economic system that cannot be controlled when it needs to be.

key point

- Trade and different types of trade
- Balance of trade and the balance of payments
- Terms of Trade
- Benefits of international trade
- Absolute Advantage and Comparative Advantage
- Limitations of the Law of Comparative Advantage
- Justifications for restricting trade
- Methods used to restrict trade
- The role of the World Trade Organization (WTO)

(i) Describe the main elements of Ireland's balance of payments (BOP) account.

(ii) Explain what is meant by a surplus on the BOP current account.

(iii) Can a surplus on the BOP current account pose problems for an economy? Explain your answer.

Marking scheme

- 3 elements @ 7 marks, 7 marks & 3 marks
- Explanation of surplus @ 7 marks
- Explanation of problem with surplus @ 6 marks (3 + 3)
- 30 marks in total

Answer

(i)

- The **Current account** comprises the trade balance (exports less imports), net income from the rest of the world, and net current transfers such as subsidies from the EU less taxes paid to the EU.
- The **Capital account** is made up of receipts and payments on one-off transactions. It includes foreign direct investment (FDI), investments in shares, and grants from the EU.
- The **Financial account** records transactions in external financial assets and liabilities. It is made up of direct investment, portfolio investment, other investment and reserve assets.

(ii) **A surplus on the current account** means that the value of exports is greater than that of imports, boosting the country's net assets by the amount of the surplus. The country is a net lender to the rest of the world.

(iii)

- **Weak domestic demand:** A country may have a surplus because of depressed demand for imports, e.g. when jobs are lost and incomes fall in a recession.
- **Over-reliance on exports:** If a country relies on exports to grow its economy, it will have a current account surplus even though its domestic economy may not be progressing.
- **Protectionism:** If a country is in surplus, other countries must have deficits. They may introduce protectionist trade measures to correct their deficits, damaging the exports of the country with the surplus.
- **Savings:** If the citizens of a country are saving money rather than spending it on imports, this will contribute to a surplus.
- **Weak currency:** To grow their exports, a country may be deliberately driving down the value of their own currency, thus causing a surplus in the balance of payments.

- **Inflation**: If exports exceed imports, the money that flows in may contribute to higher prices.
- **Capital account deficit:** A country with a current account surplus is a net lender to the rest of the world, thus making itself vulnerable to economic conditions abroad or changes in the value of foreign currencies.

2012, Section B, Question 7 (a)

The table below illustrates the Law of Comparative Advantage.

Country	Output (production per worker per week)	
	Food	Clothing
United Kingdom	40 units	10 units
China	60 units	20 units
Total Output	100 units	30 units

 (i) State the Law of Comparative Advantage.

 (ii) Explain how both countries benefit from international trade in the above example.

(iii) Calculate the terms of trade for both goods. Show your workings.

Marking scheme

- Statement of the law @ 10 marks (6 + 4)
- Explanation @ 8 marks
- Terms of trade @ 12 marks
- 30 marks in total

Answer

 (i) A country should specialise in the production of those goods and services at which it is relatively most efficient, and purchase its requirements through trade.

 (ii) If each country specialises in the production of the good at which it is relatively more efficient, we get the following result:

Country	Output (production per worker per week)	
	Food	Clothing
United Kingdom	80 units	0 units
China	0 units	40 units
Total Output	80 units	40 units

- The production of clothing has increased by 33.33%, more than the 20% fall in food production. Therefore, the world is better off than before.

or

- Given the relative value of food and clothing before trade:
  - The UK gains if it can buy a unit of clothing from China for less than 4 units of food, or in other words, more than 0.25 units of clothing for each unit of food.
  - China gains if it can buy a unit of food from the UK for less than 0.33 of a unit of clothing, or in other words, more than 3 units of food for each unit of clothing.

(iii)

UK:

- 1 unit of food is equal to 0.25 units of clothing
- 1 unit of clothing is equal to 4 units of food

China:

- 1 unit of food is equal to 0.33 units of clothing
- 1 unit of clothing is equal to 3 units of food

Possible terms of trade:

- Food lies between 0.25 and 0.3 units of clothing.
- Clothing lies between 3 and 4 units of food.

- To define population and demography
- To define the birth rate, the death rate and other population-related terms
- To explain world population trends
- To outline the uses of a census of population
- To explain the causes of emigration
- To outline the effects of emigration and immigration

Population and demography

Population refers to the number of people living in any given area, be it a town, city, country or the world in general.

- Population is counted using a **census**.
- **Demography** is the name given to the study of population.
- The **birth rate** is the number of live births per 1,000 people per year.
- The **death rate** is the number of deaths per 1,000 people per year.
- The **infant mortality** rate is the number of infant deaths (one year old or less) per 1,000 live births.
- **Life expectancy** is a statistical prediction of the number of years of life remaining at a given age. It depends on such factors as the quality of medical services, living conditions, war, natural disasters, etc. It differs greatly between countries.
- The **fertility rate** is the average number of children a woman gives birth to during her reproductive life.

- **Population density** is the average number of people living per square kilometre.
- The **dependency ratio** gives a measure of how many dependents there are in the population for every person working:

$$\frac{\text{Number of people } 0-4 \text{ years and } 65 \text{ years or over}}{\text{Number of people between } 15 \text{ and } 64 \text{ years}} \times 100$$

The higher the dependency ratio, generally the higher income tax rates have to be.

- A **natural increase** in the population occurs if births exceed deaths over a period of time.
- In addition to this, population may increase due to **net migration**, i.e. more people immigrating into a country than emigrating from it over a period of time.
- Therefore:
  - Population increase = natural increase + net migration
- On a global scale, the natural increase is the only source of population growth, but in relation to a given country, net migration is also a factor.
- **Underpopulation** exists when a rise in population would result in a rise in average income. There are more than enough economic resources to sustain current income levels.

> *exam focus*
>
> This chapter is a good example of the need to be precise in your definitions. Some of the terms found here have similar yet distinct meanings.

- **Overpopulation** exists when a rise in population would result in a fall in average income. There are currently not enough economic resources to support any more people.
- **Optimum population** exists when a rise in population would not cause average income to either rise or fall. Average income is at the highest level that current economic resources can support.

World population

- The world's population has climbed from 1 billion in 1800 to 3 billion in 1960, and is estimated to have reached roughly 7.5 billion in 2017. It is predicted to exceed 11 billion in 2100.
- Causes of this rapid growth:
  - High numbers of people of child-bearing age in **Less Developed Countries (LDCs)**
  - Earlier marital age in LDCs
  - Larger families to compensate for high infant mortality rates, and to ensure parents are cared for in old age

The census

The population of Ireland is counted every five years using a **census**. In 2016, it was measured at 4.58m people. The results have many uses:

- **Planning**: Based on the population growth in an area and its age profile, the government can plan the schools, hospitals and roads it will need in the future.
- **Labour market**: The government can identify future shortages and plan accordingly, e.g. by funding college courses.
- **Pensions**: The government can predict how many people will be over retirement age in the future, and plan accordingly.
- **Depopulation**: If an area is experiencing population decline, the government can take steps to halt it, e.g. relocate a government department there in order to create jobs.
- **Future demand**: The census gives businesses and government important information on gender, age, family size, etc. that helps in assessing future demand for goods and services.

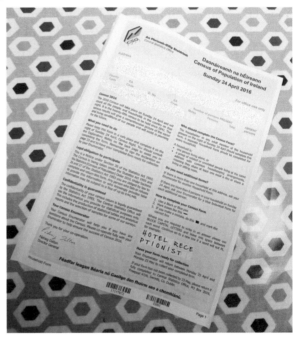

Emigration and immigration

Ireland has a long history of emigration. In 2017, about one in six people born in Ireland lived outside it. Causes of emigration fall into two broad categories:

- **Push factors**:
  - The potato famine in the late 1840s sparked a huge wave of emigration
  - Poor living conditions on small farms
  - Lack of industrial jobs in the cities
  - Political neglect: As the country was ruled by Britain, sufficient attention wasn't given to its problems. After Independence, the problem of emigration continued unabated
  - Emigration as a result of periodic recessions
- **Pull factors**:
  - Employment and opportunity in Britain and the US fueled emigration even before the Famine
  - Higher rates of pay

- An urge to see the world, present even in times of prosperity in Ireland
- The emergence of Irish communities in cities such as Liverpool and Boston provided a 'home away from home' for later Irish emigrants.

Results of emigration

- **Lower unemployment** and lower social welfare costs.
- A higher **dependency ratio**, since it is usually young people of working age who emigrate. The fewer workers who remain must support the rest of the population.
- The **smaller domestic market** hurts indigenous businesses and may cost even more jobs. It may also result in the loss of some government services that depend on economies of scale, e.g. closure of rail lines in the 1950s and 1960s.
- The resultant **lack of skilled labour** makes it harder to attract foreign investment, particularly to poorer regions.
- A **'brain drain'** occurs. The country doesn't get a return on its investment in educating those who emigrate. We lose entrepreneurs as it is often the more ambitious who emigrate. Emigrants may eventually return to Ireland as entrepreneurs, bringing new ideas with them.
- **Pressure to increase wage rates** to compete with employers abroad.
- **Loss of confidence**: Ireland naturally suffered a loss of national self-belief as a result of emigration. This can have economic consequences in terms of a lack of entrepreneurship, and an over-dependence on government help and foreign direct investment

Results of immigration

As Ireland's economy grew from the 1990s onward, we experienced significant levels of immigration, with the following results:

- A larger **domestic market**, as there is now more demand for goods and services
- Decreased **dependency ratio**, provided that the new immigrants are able to find work
- **Tax receipts** rise, as the government takes in more PAYE, PRSI, USC and VAT
- More **demand for government services**, including health and education, in turn providing more employment in those areas
- **Competition for employment** and possibly downward pressure on wage rates, as many immigrants come from countries with lower wage rates than in Ireland
- New **entrepreneurs**, as immigrants from different cultures may be more willing than Irish people to start businesses. The range of products available increases, e.g. Polish shops, Indian restaurants.

Emigration and immigration can provide topical material for Macro questions, depending on which way the trend is going in any particular year.

- Increased **house prices**, as demand grows from both owner-occupiers and those who wish to buy to rent
- **Repatriation of wages** causes a leakage from the economy, as immigrants send some of their income back to family members in their country of origin

- Definition of population and demography
- Definition of the birth rate, the death rate and other population-related terms
- World population trends
- Purpose of a census of population
- Causes of emigration
- Results of emigration and immigration

2016, Section B, Question 8 (c)
Ireland's population has become increasingly urbanised. Outline the economic consequences (positive and negative) of this development for Ireland.

Marking scheme
- 4 points @ 5 marks each (2 + 3)
- Must have at least one positive and one negative
- 20 marks in total

Answer
Positive economic consequences:

- **Use of scarce resources:** Economies of scale are achieved in the provision of services, e.g. it costs less per house to provide an electricity supply.
- **Foreign Direct Investment (FDI):** It is easier to attract multinationals to cities due to the greater availability of labour, proximity of suppliers and service providers etc. International retail chains such as Starbucks and Zara are also attracted.
- **Standard of living:** Cities generally offer more jobs, greater variety of opportunities, higher pay, public transport, etc.
- **Variety:** Larger centres of population allow for more specialised goods, services and amenities, e.g. niche restaurants, theatres, galleries, etc.
- **Entrepreneurship:** A larger market provides opportunities for more people to start businesses, e.g. landscaping, language schools etc.

Negative economic consequences:

- **Housing:** Higher house prices and rents can make moving to a city prohibitively costly.

- **Lost sense of community:** Urban societies can lack the sense of community found in rural areas. Anonymity can lead to loneliness, indifference to neighbours, and mental health issues.
- **Quality of life:** Longer commuting times, traffic jams, less green areas, higher crime rates, and air and noise pollution in urban areas can reduce the quality of life.
- **Strain on services and infrastructure:** There may be pressure on public transport, school places, parking etc.
- **Rural neglect:** Problems in country areas often receive less funding, less media attention, etc.
- **Water shortages:** Dublin is expected to face a lack of water in the future, possibly requiring water to be pumped from the Shannon.

2015, Section A, Question 9

'Since 1990 Ireland has achieved the largest gain in life expectancy for 65 year olds in all EU member states.' (The OECD Report: Health at a glance: Europe 2014)

Outline **two** possible economic implications of this development for the Irish economy **and** one policy measure the Government could consider in response to this situation.

Marking scheme

- 2 implications @ 6 marks each
- 1 policy measure @ 5 marks
- 17 marks in total

Answer

Possible economic implications:

- Reduced participation rates as more people retire
- Greater dependency ratio due to fewer people working
- Increased tax burden on the working population
- Increased need for provision of pensions
- More demand for products associated with aging
- Need for greater spending on healthcare
- People choosing to work beyond retirement, with an impact on youth employment

Policy implications:

- Make required investment in the health service
- Encourage people in the private sector to work beyond retirement age
- Extend the retirement age for the public sector
- Encourage people to contribute to pensions and to start at an early age

25 The History of Economics

aims

- To introduce the important economists and economic theories in history
- To describe each of their ideas

exam focus

The economists in this chapter are presented in chronological order, since each would have been aware of the work of those who came before. The development of any body of knowledge is a constant process of improvement on previous ideas through trial and error. New ideas can never be developed unless we are sceptical of old ones, however widely accepted.

Mercantilism

- **Thomas Mun** (1571–1641), English; **Sir James Steuart** (1712–80), Scottish
  - Precious metals are the main source of wealth.
  - Colonies are a source of precious metals and a market for exports.
  - Advocated tariffs on imports.

Physiocrats

- **François Quesnay** (1694–1774), French; **Anne-Robert-Jacques Turgot** (1727–81), French
  - Farming is the main source of wealth
  - Believed in **laissez-faire** (the government should avoid intervening in the economy), and the ownership of private property
  - Opposed protectionism and supported free trade

Classical economics

- Production is the main source of wealth.
- Believed in laissez-faire and free trade. Markets will find their own equilibrium, eliminating excess demand and supply.
- No need for government intervention except to defend the country and provide justice, education systems, etc.
- Advocated the ownership of private property.

- **Loanable funds theory** of interest rates.
- All money saved will be invested.

Adam Smith (1723–90), Scottish

- Wrote: *The Wealth of Nations* (1776)
  - The most famous classical economist, supported laissez-faire and free trade
  - Labour is the main source of wealth
  - **'The Invisible Hand'**: the self-interest of each individual is unintentionally beneficial to society. People are incentivised to help each other in order to benefit themselves.
  - Developed the **Labour Theory of Value**: The value of anything is equal to the labour it can save you.
  - Advocated specialisation of labour. This is essentially the Law of Absolute Advantage applied to individuals – concentrate on doing what you do best, and buy your other needs from other people.
  - Distinguished between productive and 'non-productive' labour, e.g. clerical workers and supervisors
  - Developed the **Canons of Taxation**
  - Advocated **Perfect Competition** as an ideal

Thomas Malthus (1766–1834), English

- Wrote: *An Essay on the Principles of Population* (1798–1826)
  - Classical economist.
  - **Iron Law of Wages**: Wages will naturally tend toward the subsistence level (just enough to get by, i.e. the equivalent of normal profit). If they get any higher, the population will rise and wages will be competed back down to the subsistence level.
  - **Theory of Population and Food Supply**: Population rises geometrically (2, 4, 8 ,16 . . .) but food supply increases arithmetically (1, 2, 3, 4 . . .), bringing inevitable disease, famine and war. He hasn't been right – yet.

Jean-Baptiste Say (1767–1832), French

- Wrote: *A Treatise on Political Economy* (1803)
  - Classical economist
  - **Say's Law**: Supply creates its own demand. If you make and manage to sell what you're good at producing, you then have the money to demand what others can produce.

David Ricardo (1772–1823), English

- Wrote: *Principles of Political Economy and Taxation* (1817)
  - Classical economist
  - Developed the **Law of Comparative Advantage** in support of free trade
  - Theory of Rent: When both good land and bad land are in use, people will pay rent to get the good land. The owners of the good land therefore earn **economic rent** (rent over and above the supply price).
  - Agreed with the Iron Law of Wages

John Stuart Mill (1806–73), English

- Wrote: *Principles of Political Economy* (1848)
  - Classical economist
  - Wrote extensively on liberty. He was guided by the principle that the individual has an absolute right to do as he wishes as long as he doesn't cause harm to others.
  - Recognised the importance of the **Law of Diminishing Marginal Returns**
  - **Wage Fund Theory**: Wages are determined by the capital fund available to pay wages divided by the working population. Wages can be increased either by cutting the population or by increasing the capital fund
  - Rejected the Labour Theory of Value, seeing supply and demand as equally important in determining value
  - Advocated a wider role for government. The excess earnings of the rich should be redistributed in order to increase the welfare of society in general.
  - Free market forces lead to inequality and thus cannot solve every problem. Intervention is also needed.
  - Correctly predicted the emergence of large companies and oligopolies due to economies of scale
  - Saw a role for trade unions in moderating the power of large companies

Karl Marx (1818–83), German

- Wrote: *The Communist Manifesto* (1848), *Das Kapital* (1867)
  - Saw a class division in society between the **proletariat** (workers) and the **bourgeoisie** (capitalists) who dominated them. He overlooked the power of trade unions to improve the rights of workers.

- Correctly predicted the emergence of oligopolies
- Falsely predicted that advances in technology would lead to mass unemployment
- Predicted a worker revolution to collectively seize the means of production, since workers generate all the income and therefore deserve all the profits. He downplayed the role of land, capital and especially enterprise in generating income and profit.
- Inspired many communist regimes, such as the Soviet Union that collapsed in 1991

Alfred Marshall (1842–1924), English

- Wrote: *Principles of Economics* (1890)
  - **Neoclassical** economist, i.e. tried to build on the ideas of earlier classical economists
  - Introduced mathematics to the study of economics
  - Invented – or discovered – **Elasticity**
  - Introduced the concept of the short and long runs
  - Introduced the concept of **Diminishing Marginal Utility**. The value of a good is based on its **Marginal Utility**, a theory still prevalent today.
  - Demand and supply act like the blades of a scissors – one cannot cut without the help of the other
  - Developed the idea of **quasi-rent**
  - Saw a role for government in the economy, particularly in limiting the power of oligopolies

John Bates Clark (1847–1938), American

- Wrote: *The Philosophy of Wealth* (1886)
  - Developed the **Marginal Productivity Theory of Wages**, i.e. an employer will keep hiring as long the marginal revenue of a worker exceeds the cost of hiring that worker

John Maynard Keynes (1883–1946), English

- Wrote: *Treatise on Money* (1930), *The General Theory of Employment, Interest and Money* (1936)
  - Neo-classical: opposed unregulated laissez-faire and believed in a larger role for government in the economy
  - Criticised classical economists for their failure to explain why recessions happen
  - An economy can be in equilibrium at less than full employment
  - Wage cuts in a recession worsen it by cutting demand
  - Government should stimulate demand in a recession by spending money (fiscal policy). The **Multiplier Effect** (which he also discovered) would ensure an even larger increase in National Income (provided it's not spent on imports) than the initial injection.

Note that since Ireland is a small and very open economy, a lot of the injection would be spent on imports, limiting its effect. Keynesian policies might work better in an economy like the US, which depends less on imports and hence has a larger multiplier.

- – Developed the **Theory of Liquidity Preference** (Chapter 16)
- – Investment is affected by expectations more than it is by the rate of interest. So not all money saved will be invested.

John Kenneth Galbraith (1908–2006), Canadian-American

- ● Wrote: *American Capitalism* (1952), *The Affluent Society* (1958), *The New Industrial State* (1967)
  - – Keynesian
  - – While recognising the ability of large companies to develop technology, he also criticised their power to persuade consumers to spend money on things they don't need
  - – Favoured taxing this spending in order to pay for public goods, e.g. highways and education
  - – Advocated government regulation of large companies to eliminate waste
  - – Advised and influenced US Presidents including John F. Kennedy (in office 1961–3) and Lyndon B. Johnson (in office 1963–9)

Milton Friedman (1912–2006), American

- ● Wrote: *A Monetary History of the United States 1867–1960* (1963), *Inflation: Causes and Consequences* (1963), *Free to Choose* (1980)
  - – A **Monetarist**, i.e. advocated use of interest rate and restricted money supply to control inflation
  - – Low inflation creates stable wages and prices, encourages investment, increases national competitiveness, and thus generates economic growth and jobs
  - – Believed that Keynes' idea of government spending in a recession would only lead to inflation
  - – Supported laissez-faire and the free market. Accused Galbraith of trying to make decisions for consumers rather than letting consumers decide.

– Fervently advocated privatisation and deregulation
– Advised US President Ronald Reagan (in office 1981–9) and influenced British Prime Minister Margaret Thatcher (in office 1979–90)
– Nobel Prize winner, 1976

Supply-side economics

- **Robert Mundell** (1932–), **Arthur Laffer** (1940–)
  - Governments should pursue policies to stimulate supply rather than demand
  - Lower marginal tax rates will encourage investment, and thus create jobs
  - The increased government revenue generated will more than make up for the tax cut
  - Regulations and other restrictions to business should be eased
  - Consumers will benefit from a greater supply of services at lower prices
  - Greater supply also keeps down inflation

Monetarism tends to be popular during times of economic growth, but when recessions come along, many turn back to Keynes.

None of the economists in this chapter were always right, although some were right more often than others. When solving economic problems – as with any problem – it helps to be pragmatic rather than ideological, i.e. **use what works** at that moment in time, not simply what you want to believe will work. As Keynes once replied to a critic: 'When the facts change, I change my mind. What do you do?' The most successful governments have used a combination of economic theories, as well as some ideas of their own.

- The main economic movements in history
- Description of each major economist's contribution

2015 Section A, Question 6
Outline two main contributions to economic thought put forward by the Classical Economists.

Marking scheme
- 9 marks (4 + 5) for first point
- 8 marks (4 + 4) for second point
- 17 marks in total

Answer

- **Free trade:** They opposed all forms of protectionism and barriers to the free movement of goods and services.
- **Laissez Faire:** They believed in limiting the role of the government in the economy to defence, security and the enforcement of legal contracts.
- **Individual freedom:** Allowing individuals to pursue their own self-interest was the best means of benefiting society.
- **Self-correcting mechanism:** A free market would more efficiently allocate resources than any government could. If demand exceeded supply or vice versa, the market would best reach equilibrium without need of government intervention.

2014, Section B, Question 8 (b) (i)
Discuss Adam Smith's four Canons of Taxation in his book, *An Inquiry into the Nature and Causes of the Wealth of Nations* (1776).

Marking scheme

- 4 points of information @ 6 marks each
- Total: 24 marks

Answer

- **Equity:** The higher a person's income, the greater should be the percentage they pay in tax. This is called a progressive tax system, as it places a greater burden on those with a greater ability to pay.
- **Economy:** The cost of collecting tax should be a small proportion of the tax collected, i.e. the bulk of the tax collected should be made available for government spending.
- **Certainty:** The rates of taxation and the amount to be paid should be clear to the taxpayer, allowing them greater scope to plan their spending. Similarly the government will have a better idea of how much tax it is likely to collect and can also plan accordingly. In addition, tax rates should only be revised at fixed and well known intervals, e.g. annually.
- **Convenience:** The process of collecting tax should not be disruptive to the taxpayer, e.g. PAYE is collected at source by the employer and passed on to the Revenue Commissioners.

26 The European Union

- To define the European Union (EU)
- To provide a brief history of the EU
- To describe the main EU institutions
- To explain how EU decisions are implemented
- To outline the main elements of the Common Agricultural Policy (CAP) and the Common Fisheries Policy
- To explore the impact of Brexit on Ireland
- To discuss the advantages and disadvantages of Ireland's membership of the Euro
- Criticisms of the EU

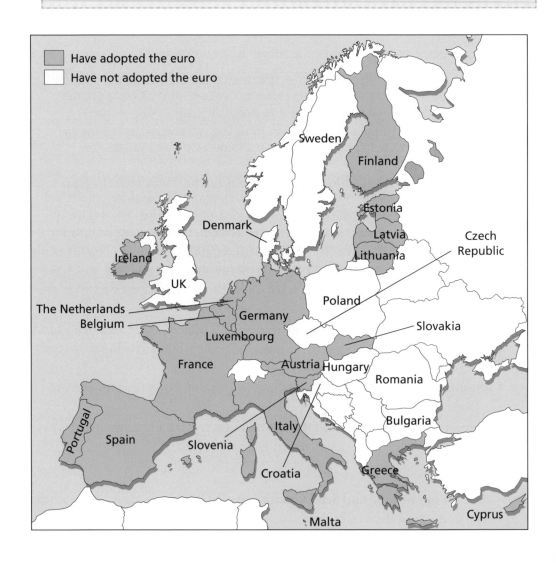

The European Union

The **European Union** is an economic and political union of 28 countries and over 500 million citizens that co-operates closely on a range of economic, social and political issues.

- It has developed a **single market**, i.e. freedom of movement of goods, services, capital and labour, in addition to a common external tariff.
- It has common policies on agriculture, fisheries, regional development and other issues.
- 19 of its members have a common currency, the Euro.
- It has some common defence and foreign policies.

Implications of the Single European Market (SEM)

- **Freedom of movement** of goods, services, capital and labour across the EU (much like in the US).
- **Larger market**: Irish firms can sell their produce unhindered in any EU member state.
- **Foreign competition**: Likewise any EU producer can sell their goods and services in Ireland.
  - Increases the variety of goods available to Irish consumers
  - Irish firms forced to become more competitive, which in turn increases exports and employment
  - Places small Irish producers under threat, e.g. the Irish fishing industry
- **Economies of scale**: Firms make cost savings, hopefully passing them on to consumers in the form of lower prices.
- **Public procurement**: Competition for government contracts is open to all firms in the EU and not just those of the member state concerned, e.g. the building of motorways.
- **Product standards**: States have negotiated common product standards and regulations, allowing them to be traded across the EU. This process is continuing.
- **Recognition of qualifications**: This makes it easier for a citizen of any member state to work in any other member state. They also do not lose their rights to social welfare payments.
- **Single Passport in Banking and Insurance**: This is intended to allow banks and insurance companies to operate in any member state while still being controlled by the Regulator in their home country.
- **Cohesion funds**: States are given financial help in order to qualify for entry to the Euro.
- **Foreign Direct Investment (FDI)**: In order to access the EU single market, many firms from outside the EU have chosen to locate in Ireland.

History of the European Union

1951: The **European Coal and Steel Community (ECSC)** was established as a 'first step in the federation of Europe'.

- It was thought that if European countries worked more closely together, the likelihood of a repeat of wars like World War II would be reduced.
- There were six founding members: Belgium, France, Italy, Luxembourg, the Netherlands, and West Germany.

1957: The **European Economic Community (EEC)** was established in the **Treaty of Rome**.

- It had the same six founding members as the ECSC.
- It was initially a **customs union**, i.e. a **free trade area** (freedom of movement of goods and services) with a common external tariff.

1973: **Ireland**, the United Kingdom and Denmark joined.

1979: The first directly elected European Parliament.

1981: Greece joined.

1986: Spain and Portugal joined.
The Single European Act. This set a goal of establishing a single market by the end of 1992.

1990: German re-unification brought the former East Germany into the EEC.

1993: The **Treaty of Maastricht**. This began the process of establishing the Euro. The EEC was renamed the European Union (EU), since it was no longer simply an economic union. EU citizenship was introduced.

1995: Austria, Finland and Sweden joined.

1999: The Euro was launched as Austria, Belgium, Finland, France, Germany, Ireland, Italy, Luxembourg, the Netherlands, Portugal and Spain locked their exchange rates.
The **Treaty of Amsterdam**. This gave more power to the Parliament, and made the Commission more accountable.

2001: Greece joined the Euro.

2002: Euro notes and coins were introduced.

2003: The **Treaty of Nice**. This reformed the institutions in preparation for the further enlargement of the EU. It also began the move away from unanimous decision-making, reflecting the larger membership of the EU.

2004: Cyprus, the Czech Republic, Estonia, Hungary, Latvia, Lithuania, Malta, Poland, Slovakia and Slovenia joined.

2007: Bulgaria and Romania joined the EU, bringing the membership to 27. Slovenia joined the Euro.

2008: Cyprus and Malta joined the Euro.

2009: The **Treaty of Lisbon**. It continued the move away from unanimous decision-making. It created the position of President of the European Council and the *Charter of Fundamental Rights of the European Union*. It unified the previous treaties.

2009: Slovakia joined the Euro.

2011: Estonia joined the Euro, bringing Eurozone membership to 17.

2013: Croatia joined the EU, bringing total membership to 28.

2014: Latvia joined the Euro.

2015: Lithuania joined the Euro, bringing Eurozone membership to 19.

2016: The UK voted to leave the EU, a process scheduled to be complete in 2019.

The main institutions of the European Union

- The **European Parliament** sits in Strasbourg and Brussels. It is made up of 751 **Members of the European Parliament (MEPs)** directly elected by the voters of the EU every five years.

  > Ireland is the only EU country that ratifies EU treaties by means of a referendum. Both the Nice and Lisbon treaties were rejected by the Irish people before being accepted in later referenda. Our relationship with the EU is a topical issue in Ireland. Exam questions may therefore focus on the pros and cons of various aspects of the EU.

  - It shares legislative and budgetary authority with the Council of Ministers.
  - It approves the appointment of the EU Commission and supervises its operation.
  - It advises the Council of Ministers.
  - It appoints the EU Ombudsman.
  - It deals with issues that affect all states.

- The **Council of the European Union (Council of Ministers)** sets the political objectives of the EU and takes the final decision on all new laws.
  - It is the main decision-making body of the EU.
  - It shares legislative and budgetary power with the Parliament. It enacts legislation through regulations, directives and decisions.
  - It co-ordinates the policies of member states, including their broad economic policies, and resolves differences between them.
  - Its meetings are attended by the 28 national ministers responsible for the topic under discussion, e.g. finance or agriculture.
  - Votes are taken by either majority or unanimity with votes allocated according to population.
  - Twice a year, the heads of government – making up the **Council of Europe** – meet in an EU summit. They are responsible for defining the general political direction and priorities of the Union. Since 2009, the Council of Europe has had a permanent President.

- The **European Commission** is the main body responsible for running the EU.
  - It is the executive of the European Union and promotes its general interest.
  - It has the sole power to propose new EU laws.
  - It makes sure that EU treaties and laws are obeyed.
  - It is independent of national governments.
  - Each member state nominates one member to the commission for a period of five years. They must be approved by the Parliament.

- It manages the day-to-day business of the EU.
- It proposes the EU budget.
- It negotiates international trade agreements on behalf of the EU.
- It is accountable to the Parliament.

- The **Court of Justice of the European Union (CJEU)** ensures that EU law is observed in all member states.
  - It interprets EU law for member states, companies and EU citizens.
  - Its rulings ensure that everyone has the same understanding of the EU treaties, regulations and directives.
- The **Court of Auditors** ensures that taxpayer funds from the budget of the European Union have been correctly spent.
  - The auditors prepare an annual report.
  - They provide Parliament and the Council with a statement of assurance certifying that the accounts are reliable, and that the operations to which they relate are legal and regular.
  - They perform spot checks, and work to prevent fraud.
  - They advise on how EU finances could be better managed and made more accountable to the citizens.
  - The goal is to ensure that taxpayers get value for money.

exam focus

If you think the EU is complicated, you're right. If you think it doesn't matter, you're wrong. More than 75% of all laws that come into force in Ireland every year come not from Dublin, but from Brussels and Strasbourg.

Once a proposal is adopted, it is implemented in one of three ways:

- **Regulations**: These apply immediately across the EU without the need for laws to be passed in each member state.
- **Directives**: These must be implemented in each country, but the way in which this is done is decided by country.
- **Decisions**: These can be addressed towards particular countries, individuals or companies, and are binding.

The CAP

The **Common Agricultural Policy (CAP)** is an EU common policy with a stated goal to provide farmers with a reasonable standard of living, consumers with quality food at fair prices and to preserve rural heritage. It involves:

- A **single market** for farm produce in the EU
- Direct payments to farmers based on production that meets consumer demand, and linked with environmental sustainability ('greening'), animal health and welfare, and food safety
- Tariffs and quotas on certain goods from outside the EU
- Training of young farmers

Criticisms of the CAP

- It restricts imports from **Less Developed Countries (LDCs)** that depend far more on agricultural output than the EU does.
- It results in higher food prices, due to the lack of competition from outside the EU. Food constitutes a larger proportion of the spending of poorer households.
- Subsidies in the past caused production to far exceed consumption.
- Excess supply was dumped on Third World markets, further impoverishing farmers in LDCs.
- It requires higher taxation to fund it.
- The CAP takes up a large proportion (approximately 40%) of the EU budget, and could be better spent elsewhere.
- Most of the payments go to a minority of farmers, though this is being addressed.

The common fisheries policy

The **Common Fisheries Policy** sets out the EU's approach to regulating fisheries in EU waters. Its goals include:

- Ensuring sustainable exploitation of marine life
- Minimising the impact of fishing on marine eco-systems
- Providing a fair standard of living for those who depend on fishing
- Creating competition across the EU fishing industry. Ireland's fishing industry has been heavily impacted by the entry of larger foreign trawlers into Irish waters.
- Ensuring that the interests of consumers are a priority

Impact of Brexit

Advantages for Ireland

- If the EU imposes tariffs on the UK, Irish exports will become more competitive within the EU.
- Ireland will gain jobs and investment if UK firms relocate here in order to maintain access to the EU market. As the only English-speaking country not just in the Eurozone but in the EU, Ireland can attract other non-EU multinationals for the same reason.

Disadvantages for Ireland

- EU tariffs on imports from the UK would make them more expensive.
- If the UK imposes tariffs on imports from Ireland, this will reduce our exports to the UK, costing Ireland jobs in the process.
- Given the Republic's border with Northern Ireland and the strong economic links between the two, our economy is additionally vulnerable.
- Any decline in the British economy resulting from Brexit would also hurt Irish exports to the UK, in turn affecting employment.
- It is hoped that Brexit will not affect Irish people's ability to live and work in the UK, something we have long taken for granted.
- To attract and maintain FDI the UK may cut its corporation tax, drawing investment and jobs away from Ireland.
- Because the UK has been an important contributor to the budget of the EU, the Irish agriculture industry, as well as other recipients of EU spending, are likely to be negatively affected.
- EU regulations will no longer apply in the UK. Differing standards would create administrative barriers to trade and labour mobility, e.g. goods ordered from the UK will no longer be covered by EU consumer law.
- The Pound has weakened since the Brexit vote. Irish exports to the UK have lost competitiveness. Retailers here have lost business as shopping in Northern Ireland or online from Britain is now cheaper.
- Since no country has previously left the EU, no-one knows exactly what its effects will be, and some even doubt that the UK will eventually go through with Brexit. Such uncertainty causes investors to delay decisions, reducing trade, jobs and economic growth.
- An influx of UK firms to Ireland would add to residential and commercial property prices and rents, and increase traffic congestion and inflation.
- The European Health Insurance card will no longer be valid in the UK.
- Brexit may encourage other countries to contemplate leaving the EU.

The Euro

Ireland joined the single currency in 1999. Notes and coins came into use at the beginning of 2002. This is referred to as an **Economic and Monetary Union (EMU)**.

Advantages of Ireland's membership of the Euro

- Exchange rate risk is removed. Businesses can buy and sell on credit with greater confidence.
- It is easier to compare prices between member countries, thus encouraging competition.
- A single currency for a single market makes sense.
- Currency speculation is eliminated.
- Transaction costs fall for both businesses and consumers.
- There is increased trade between Eurozone countries.
- There is increased foreign investment, especially from US companies which want an English-speaking base in the Eurozone.
- Support from the ECB if we fall into financial difficulty.

Disadvantages of Ireland's membership of the Euro

- The UK – one of our biggest trading partners – chose to remain outside the Euro. Since the UK voted in 2016 to leave the EU, the prospect of it joining the Euro receded further.
- In a recession, we need low interest rates to assist recovery. In a boom, we need higher interest rates to dampen inflation. As part of the Euro, however, Ireland gets the same interest rate as the rest of the Eurozone whether it suits us or not.
- We cannot devalue to correct a balance of payments deficit.
- A common currency with a common monetary policy has led to the need for closer fiscal coordination between the Eurozone countries.

Criticisms that have been levelled at the EU

- Too centralised and bureaucratic
- Undemocratic and ignores the people
- Reduces national sovereignty
- Language and cultural barriers still barriers to a true single market
- Should confine itself to being an economic union, not a political one
- The CAP distorts trade

key point

- Purpose of the European Union
- History of the European Union
- Main EU institutions and their functions
- How EU decisions are implemented
- The Common Agricultural Policy (CAP) and the Common Fisheries Policy
- The impact of Brexit on Ireland
- Advantages and disadvantages of the Euro for Ireland
- Criticisms of the EU

2014, Section A, Question 6
Outline two possible economic effects for the Irish Economy of the euro (€) appreciating in value against the US dollar ($).

Marking scheme

- 10 marks for 1st correct answer
- 7 marks for 2nd correct answer
- 17 marks in total

Answer

- **Less tourists travelling to Ireland.** Less Americans would holiday in Ireland because their dollar would now buy less Euro. Conversely, it would become more attractive for Irish people to travel to America.

- **Fall in the price of imports.** Since the euro would now buy more dollars, imports from the United States would be cheaper in Euro terms, which would make them more competitive, in turn hurting Irish firms dependent on the domestic market.

- **Rise in the price of exports.** Goods exported from Ireland would become more expensive in dollar terms and therefore less competitive.

If an exam question asks about the Euro *falling* in value, the results would be the opposite of each of the points above. As you study past exam questions, bear in mind how they can alternate in this fashion.

- **Reduction in employment.** Ireland depends on exports. If they fall, jobs are likely to be lost in industries that depend on exports to the United States.

- **Less American investment in Ireland.** Since the dollar buys less euro, Ireland would not be as attractive as an investment opportunity. On the other hand, Irish firms may become more interested in investing in the United States, where the returns would now be greater.

Section A, Question 5, 2007
Outline THREE functions / responsibilities of the European Central Bank (ECB).

Marking scheme

- 6 marks for first function, 5 marks each for two additional functions
- 16 marks in total

Answer

- **Implement monetary policy:** The ECB has the power to set interest rates, control the money supply and the availability of credit and hence protect the value of the euro.

- **Ensure Price Stability:** In response to changes in the inflation rate, the ECB will adjust the interest rate in order to keep prices steady and hence encourage economic growth.

- **Supervise the financial industry:** The ECB, via the national central banks, regulates all financial institutions in the Eurozone.

- **Issue euro notes and coin:** The ECB has the sole authority to issues euro currency within the Eurozone.

- **Manages official external reserves:** The ECB manages the Eurozone's holdings of foreign currencies, gold, and other reserves held as security against the issue of the euro.

27 Economic Growth and Development

- To define economic growth
- To outline its advantages and disadvantages
- To define economic development
- To define and discuss the characteristics of Less Developed Countries (LDCs)
- To outline Rostow's stages of economic development

Economic growth

Economic growth is an increase in GNP per capita *without* a change in the structure of society.

Advantages of economic growth

- Better standard of living
- More employment and opportunity
- Emigrants have the chance to return home
- Improved balance of payments
- Greater freedom and choice
- Higher government revenue to fund public services and improvements in infrastructure
- Reduced poverty, reduced dependency on outside help

Disadvantages of economic growth

- Damage to the environment
- Benefits aren't shared equally
- Stressful, materialistic society
- Sense of community can be lost
- Opportunity cost of growth: Current expenditure must be foregone in order to invest in future growth
- Over-crowded urban areas, under-inhabited rural areas
- Money makes things possible, but it cannot buy happiness

As Ireland has gone from boom to bust in the first decade of the 21st century, the advantages and disadvantages of economic growth have become a very topical source of exam questions.

Economic development

Economic development is an increase in GNP per capita *accompanied by* a change in the structure of society.

LDCs

A **Less Developed Country (LDC)** is one that exhibits the lowest indicators of socioeconomic development. It has the following characteristics:

- **High dependence on the primary sector**: Farming, mining, etc. Underdeveloped industrial and services sectors, very small services sector.
- **Poor living conditions**: Substandard housing, water and sewage systems.
- **Low life expectancy**: Due to famine, war, natural disasters, HIV/AIDS, poor health system, etc.
- **High birth rates,** resulting in a rapidly expanding population, which puts pressure on public services.
- **Overdependence on one export,** e.g. coffee, copper, etc. Countries like this are nicknamed a 'banana republic'.
- **Political problems**: Dictators, rigged elections, frequent coups and civil wars, high military spending, crime.
- **Economic dualism**: The elite who rule the country and make money from its chief export are rich; everyone else is poor. There is very little social mobility.
- **Education**: Low literacy rates, limited education system. These factors impede further development.
- **Poor infrastructure**: Poor transport system and electricity network, infrequent international air access.

- **A low level of saving**: A country that cannot afford to save will find it very difficult to invest without outside help.
- **Foreign debt**: LDCs have to borrow heavily from banks in the developed world in order to invest in infrastructure.
- **Poor terms of trade**: Their exports sell at a low price, but what they need to import costs them a higher price.
- **Multinationals**: Foreign companies can dictate to LDCs regarding wage rates, tax rates and labour laws.
- **High dependence on foreign aid**, which can be stolen, or sold by the government, before it reaches its destination.

LDCs cannot make progress without change in several key areas:

- **Infrastructure**: LDCs need electrical and communication systems, housing, water, sanitation and better roads.
- **Education**: LDCs initially require literacy and numeracy skills, and knowledge of better agricultural techniques. If the industrial and services sectors can be developed, then the education system can be expanded to support them.
- **Political reform**: Little progress is possible without an end to corruption, and civil and tribal warfare. There is little immediate prospect of this in many LDCs.
- **Debt**: LDCs owe billions of Euro to lenders in America and Europe that could be better spent at home. In recent years there have been campaigns to have these debts forgiven. While of great assistance, forgiving debt may also encourage LDCs to borrow irresponsibly in the future.

LDCs are always in the news, and hence give the examiners topical material for Macro questions.

- **Aid**: Even as they try to progress economically, LDCs will still be heavily dependent on foreign aid for the foreseeable future. Ireland is committed to donating 0.7% of its GNP, but currently gives only about half of this.

Rostow's stages of economic development

- **Traditional society**
  - High dependence on subsistence agriculture
  - Primitive farming methods
  - Self-sufficient; very little imports or exports
  - Low output per worker
  - Little or no manufacturing or services
  - Poor infrastructure
  - Country run by elite minority of landowners
  - Conservative culture distrustful of change
- **Preconditions for take-off**
  - More awareness of the benefits of improvements in farming methods and technology
  - Desire to emulate more affluent societies
  - Culture becomes more hopeful of change
  - Infrastructure improves, facilitating trade
  - Agricultural output increases, exports increase
  - Larger incomes allow saving and hence investment
  - Industrialisation begins
- **Take-off**
  - Greater application of technology in farming sector
  - Continued investment in industrial sector
  - Production becomes more capital intensive
  - Migration to cities to work in factories
  - Fall in numbers employed in agriculture
  - Emergence of services sector
  - Infrastructure develops further
  - Incomes rise, and consumer demand rises too
  - Economic growth becomes self-sustaining
- **Drive to maturity**
  - Continued rise in investment and incomes
  - Diversification of industry as new industries replace traditional ones
  - Import substitution
  - Continued urbanisation
  - Government expands public services and social welfare

- **Age of mass consumption**
  - Services sector overtakes manufacturing sector
  - High income per capita
  - Expansion of suburbs
  - Development of electronic infrastructure
- **Post-industrial society (added after Rostow)**
  - Greater sophistication in manufacturing
  - Preference for more leisure time
  - Growing emphasis on the quality of life
  - More spending on health, welfare and further education
  - Greater concern for the effects of development on the environment

Problems with Rostow's theory

- Development rarely follows a clear, inevitable path.
- Countries often progress a little and then stagnate.
- Each country faces a unique set of problems.
- Investment doesn't have to come from within a country.

Regurgitating theory might get you a H4 or even a H3, but a H2 or H1 depends on critical thinking – being able to form your own opinion and back it up, and being able to see both sides of an argument. Rostow's theory is one example.

key point

- Definition of economic growth
- Advantages and disadvantages of economic growth
- Definition of economic development
- Characteristics of Less Developed Countries (LDCs)
- Rostow's stages of economic development

exam Q

2014, Section B, Question 7 (a)
 (i) Distinguish between the terms 'economic development' and 'economic growth' with reference to Less Developed Countries (LDCs).
 (ii) Outline three characteristics of LDCs.

Marking scheme
- 2 definitions @ 5 marks each.
- 3 characteristics @ 5 marks each (2 + 3).
- 25 marks in total.

Answer

(i)

- **Economic Development** is an increase in GNP per person in a country, accompanied by a change in the structure of society.
- **Economic Growth** is an increase in GNP per person without any changes in the structure of society.

(ii)

- High dependence on the primary sector, underdeveloped industrial and services sectors, very small services sector.
- Poor housing, water and sanitary systems.
- Low literacy rates, which holds back education and development.
- High population growth, which stretches government services beyond their limits.
- Low life expectancy due to famine, war, natural disasters, HIV/AIDS, poor health system etc.
- Overdependence on one export.
- Dictatorships, corruption, rigged elections, civil unrest, high military spending, and high crime rates.
- Poor infrastructure: Poor transport system and electricity network, infrequent international air access.
- Multi-national companies can dictate to LDCs regarding wage rates, tax rates, labour and environmental regulations.
- Very little investment: A country that cannot afford to save will find it very difficult to purchase capital goods.
- Little social mobility: The government and economy are controlled by an elite; everyone else is poor.
- Foreign debt: LDCs have to borrow heavily from banks in the developed world in order to invest in infrastructure.
- Poor terms of trade: Exports sell at a low price, import must be purchased at a higher price.
- High dependence on foreign aid.

2014, Section B, Question 7 (a)

(i) Describe three types of foreign aid available to LDCs.

(ii) Discuss why foreign aid may not always result in economic growth in LDCs.

Marking scheme

- 3 types @ 5 marks each
- 2 reasons @ 5 marks each
- 25 marks in total

Answer

(i)

- **National debt restructuring:** If a LDC's national debt is cancelled or the interest payments are reduced or the payment period lengthened, money is freed up for spending on education and infrastructure.

- **Training and technology:** By training workers in LCD and providing them with vital technology, productivity increases.

- **Direct financial aid:** Governments in developed countries can directly fund infrastructure, education, and health projects in LDCs, in addition to providing funding in emergency situations such as famine.

- **Voluntary agencies:** Non-Government Organisations (NGOs) also provide funding, training, etc. to LDCs.

- **Foreign citizens:** By choosing to spend time working in LDCs, by purchasing 'fair trade' products from LDCs, by shopping in charity shops, or by donating food, clothes, used mobile phones etc. to LDCs, ordinary people around the world can make a difference.

- **Multinationals:** If firms from the developed world locate factories in LDCs, they can create employment, raise skill levels, boost exports and increase tax revenue for the government that can in turn be invested in infrastructure.

- **Trade:** Improved terms of trade and greater access to markets in the developed world would allow LDCs to earn higher prices for their produce, increase exports, and raise their standard of living.

(ii)

- **Unequal distribution of wealth:** The ruling elite may be the only ones who profit from the aid while the vast majority remain in poverty. Aid should not be diverted into non-productive military spending or into vanity projects such as palaces at the expense of the schools or hospitals where it is really needed.

- **Culture of dependence:** Giving aid, while of obvious immediate benefit, also creates expectations of further aid in the future. This may impede the self-reliance and entrepreneurship needed for more sustainable development.

- **Rapid population growth:** If the growth of aid in is outmatched by population growth, the LDC will continue to experience difficulty.

- **Costs to the environment:** A downside of economic aid is the pollution, deforestation and urban sprawl that can accompany the economic development it is intended to support.